Tokyo
City and Architecture

Livio Sacchi

Introduction by
Franco Purini

Art editor
Franco Mercuri

Universe

Design
Marcello Francone

Editorial Coordination
Vincenza Russo

Layout
Paola Ranzini

Translations
Globe s.r.l., Foligno

First published in the United States of America in 2004 by
Universe Publishing
A Division of Rizzoli International Publications, Inc.
300 Park Avenue South
New York, NY 10010

www.rizzoliusa.com

Originally published in Italy in 2004 by
Skira Editore S.p.A.
Palazzo Casati Stampa
via Torino 61
20123 Milano
Italy

www.skira.net

2004 2005 2006 / 10 9 8 7 6 5 4 3 2 1

ISBN 0-7893-1212-3

Library of Congress Catalogue Control Number 2004108867

Printed in Italy

Contents

Introduction
Franco Purini

The Future's Future

For some years now Tokyo has been the capital of the third Grand Tour. The first focused on Rome, in which 18th and 19th-century Northern European intellectuals and artists saw the highest exponent of ancient splendor, as well as the regenerative force of the exotic. The second Grand Tour was staged in the boundless territories of the United States; the hub was New York City, the great symbol of progress, the magic gateway to a land of freedom and adventure, where every dream could come true. Today, fueled by globalism, the endless Japanese metropolis has become the climax of a new cognitive and highly imaginative itinerary, a third Grand Tour, this time in the world's most emergent area. The focus of the world has moved to China and Japan, Korea and Malaysia, and Tokyo is the pivot of this geographical quadrant, even though competition from Hong Kong, Seoul, Singapore and especially Shanghai is getting more and more intense. The secret of Tokyo's allure is that, as in William Gibson's writings, it offers an enthralling vision of the *future's future*. Moreover, in Japan, and in the Far East in general, anything that is associated with *the newest of the new* seems to stem directly from tradition, in a sort of mystic melding of all time.

In 1960, when Kenzō Tange produced his plan for the expansion of Tokyo out over its vast bay, the city gained consciousness of the reach it had attained: a place where growth strategies thrive, and where a utopian vision was combined with extreme forms of urbanization based on the colonization of gigantic megastructures built over the water. In 1964, this world dimension was validated at the Olympic Games, a great media success. Next, Frank Lloyd Wright's Imperial Hotel was demolished in 1968. A few years earlier, the building had appeared too sumptuous and gloomy to Dino Buzzati, with its dark bricks separated by layers of golden mortar. Now, without it, Tokyo was free of the building that epitomized Japan's debt to modern architecture. Once rid of this weighty evidence, which had led Hokusai's native land to play an essentially limited, if prestigious, role as a precursor, and spurred by recent aseismatic regulations that finally allowed buildings to soar upwards, Tokyo could at last take on New York and surpass it.

On first step into urban Tokyo, the traveler from Europe, or the more advanced regions of the West, may undergo visual trauma. The city spreads in successive waves in an infinite, chaotic mass of different yet curiously similar buildings that are almost like three-dimensional evolutions of the ideograms that cover them. The minute and the colossal follow one another and clash in a powerful energetic flow that knows no rest, while tangled strips of infrastructure wind between the buildings in spectacular spatial combinations. All is bathed in a hazy, dim light, which rarely brightens, and permeates every interstice of the city, from window to window, sign to sign and corner to corner. At night, artificial lighting transforms Tokyo into a fantastical apparition of artificial mountain ranges that glow like braziers. The visual trauma is due to Tokyo giving no sense of any recognizable structure. Compared with Europe, or the West in general, where cities still have a perceptible—albeit residual and fragmentary—*urban form* which is always based on a more or less rational *order*, in Tokyo you find a randomness in which every urban rule is overturned or negated. Or at least so it seems. As a matter of fact, once initial impressions have been overcome, you begin to notice the presence of recurring threads in the urban fabric, first on a subliminal level, than more consciously; a fabric made of multiple, fractal agglomerates of settlements. These agglomerates are grouped in *self-similar masses*, suggesting urban spaces which are not defined by clearly scaled hierarchies or distinct morphological types. Here, urban spatiality seems to feature the unplanned coexistence of architectural units and the incidental contiguity of what is small and large, simple and complex, uniform and variable. A homogeneous, pervasive—though immaterial—*rhythm* beats over everything, constituting an amazing unifying element in its almost hypnotic repetition of the same model. In this sense you discover that in the end Tokyo is a simple city that is different from European and American cities only because urban planning is practically absent. If the former are *cities of space*, governed by the laws of perspective, then Tokyo is a *city of situations*. It is a city in which no two points are the same, which demands that those who traverse it develop dynamic, changeable mental maps where the interpenetration of volumes, the intensity of relationships, and the connection between distant and even opposite levels in the urban text assume an essential role. If, as Walter Benjamin wrote, you can lose your bearings in a western city, but only after lengthy exploration of its layout, which even when highly stratified is always logical, then in Asia's greatest city you are completely disorientated right from the start. It is not like in New York or Paris, where you lose control of the city; here you feel the city is totally indifferent to you. You are just an extra in an urban representation where the individual is completely transcended as is the immense metropolitan mass in which he dissolves, in a sort of ecstatic annihilation.

The reading of Tokyo that Livio Sacchi offers in this work is in complete accord with what the city itself wants to reveal. The interpretation follows the urban processes in their most recognizable and communicable manifestations, and leads to an almost total identification with whatever is being described. The metaphor of the liquidity of space; the analogy between the urban environment and the digital universe, from which comes the consistency of the city with the virtual world; the labyrinthine essence of the city—all of this is taken to the letter, while simultaneously hiding a more elementary reality. This emerges from expansive logistics that delineate a hard, separatist metropolis, marked by invisible but effective barriers, and crossed by harsh architectural and social conflicts in deep contrast with the free, endless flow of people, information and images. From this point of view, in their establishment as a *constant*, even the processes of body hybridization and metamorphosis—fostered by electronics—reveal themselves much less clear and unpredictable than they appear.

Livio Sacchi's wide-ranging, detailed reflections focus on the central question of whether the Nipponese metropolis represents the last phase of the contemporary city's degeneration or if it is instead the first example of a new type of human settlement: hyperbolic, simultaneous *post-cities* which have already become actual *geographical phenomena*. These are boundless masses whose physical substance will be less and less determinant, reaching a relative *invisibility*, while communicative processes and self-representational mechanisms acquire primary significance. In the first case, the most suitable interpretative model of the city would be an aesthetic—and we might say *terminal*—restoration, full of anthropological recollections and inter-contaminations with other languages; in the second, an evolutional, grass-roots decodification of the new urban organisms would prevail. *Tokyo* is suspended between the two extremes, and this ambivalence is what makes it so interesting; the reader may choose which mode he prefers. This book does not only provide an understanding of Tokyo, split into its various components and then recomposed, but the detailed analysis of the city creates a better understanding of all global cities, almost foreshadowing their imminent, mutual *crossing*, in the true sense of the one being contained in the other.

Like the city it describes, the structure of the book is an interwoven, interacting sequence of narrative blocks in which historical reconstruction, references to relevant literature, in-depth theoretical studies and allusions to the evolution of customs alternate and combine in a mobile mosaic, creating an agile, comprehensive *hypertext*. This book is written in simple, lucid prose, which nevertheless avoids any kind of popularizing simplification and penetrates the most intricate nodes of the topic with illuminating competence. Furthermore, it is enhanced by a great number of original, relevant illustrations, and it offers the key to delineating the next changes Tokyo will undergo rather than being purely restricted to the present. This work by Livio Sacchi fills an important gap in urban writings, offering a portrait of what is currently the planet's most important metropolis, along with an enthralling model of how the global city can be perceived and understood today.

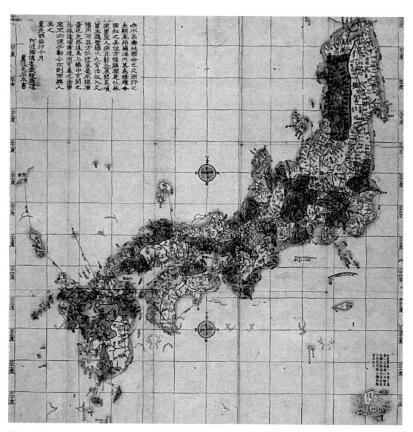

Map of Japan, 1783

Ishmael, Herman Melville's hero in Moby Dick, says:
"If that double-bolted land, Japan, is ever to become hospitable,
it is the whale-ship alone to whom the credit will be due; for already
she is on the threshold." This was in 1851.
If, over a century and a half later, Japan is now an open, hospitable
country, it may also be thanks to the venturesome whale-ships from
Nantucket the novel refers to. But Japan still remains a far-off island,
and many still consider its ancient yet brand new culture "double-bolted."

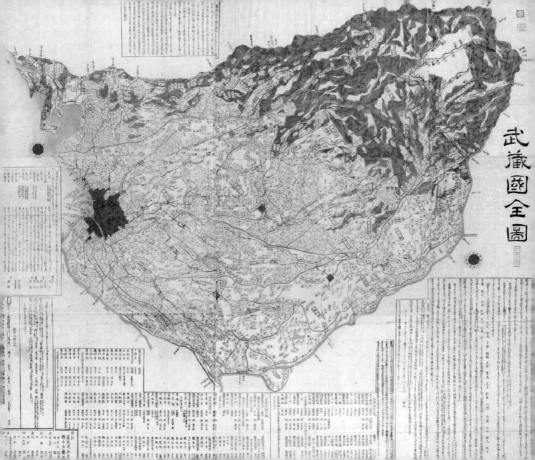

1. The Global City

Tokyo is today the largest city in the developed world. In our case, although the term "city" will probably sound inadequate and obsolete, we are applying it simply out of habit, and because no more appropriate word exists. It may be no chance that written Japanese avails itself of a single ideogram for two different concepts: "market" ("ichi"), and "city" ("shi"). Hence, Tokyo is more a place of trade than a "civitas," or a community of inhabitants.

If, for instance, your first visit to Tokyo were to take place in the evening, in the heart of Shinjuku or Shibuya, you might think you had landed in another time, on another planet. The city image is very different from what we are used to in Europe, America or even other parts of Asia. This is true in spite of the extensive process of globalization, and thus of standardization, we are now being subjected to. You experience a deep cultural and visual shock: Tokyo appears vast, uncontrollable, incomprehensible, chaotic, ugly.

This is probably why it is relatively unpopular with tourists. Any previous experience is of little help when it comes to orientating yourself: it is so completely different from European cities—and resembles American ones only in its impressive infrastructure and extreme verticality—that it systematically evades any easy comparison. The urban structure differs so greatly from that of Western cities that for visitors in general and architects alike visual perception is understandably difficult; yet, this sense of unease is more psychological than practical.

In this regard, Alberto Arbasino wrote: "Tokyo is fairly horrendous; like Los Angeles, but worse, since spasmodic overcrowding presses down on an overblown structure . . . streets and highways cross irregular, enervating openings between immense office skyscrapers that still glare blatantly well after nightfall . . . dried-up gardens, scattered shops, suddenly jammed streets, absurdly rural alleys, and buildings made with nothing but cheap, perishable materials, such as wood, dull metal and crumbling concrete, in a scene of boundless desolation."[1] Cesare Brandi was just as disgusted: "Tokyo is a frightening city, the largest and ugliest in the world . . . urban planning is chaotic, nonexistent. Like the dragons of Japanese legends—dragons that have now become functional—high overpasses climb over one another; at some points, where as many as three wind overhead, they look like a caricature of some of Piranesi's obsessive prisons."[2]

Nevertheless, with time this perception is destined to change. Little by little, the city offers a different face, as one discovers its richness, reliability, efficiency, dynamism, experimentalism, cleanliness, safety, kind-

Kikuchi Shuzo, Utagawa and Sadahide, *Musashi no kuni zenzu*, Map of the Tokyo region, 1858

ness, sensitivity, culture and even beauty. It is a beauty that can only be understood in the Japanese sense of the term, which entails patience. It is therefore—also—an aesthetic appreciation, although it might be motivated by prosaic reasoning that conceals disquieting aspects: "people could not forever deem ugly a city which, ousting New York, has become in the 1980s the richest and most powerful on earth."[3]

Tokyo is today one of the few global cities that, along with London, New York and maybe one or two others, forms part of a true transnational system. It is also an amazing capital of contemporary architecture and constitutes an exceptional urban phenomenon which has undergone very rapid transformations; it is, in other words, to be observed with great attention.

In this context, Vittorio Gregotti observes: "In the past years, literature and films have given us a significantly indirect picture of the way in which such contradictions in the city's transformation can become highly expressive, and thus help reconstruct a new, violated identity for the country. Naturally, in order to understand this, the other face of Japan must not be forgotten: today, from a technological and productive point of view, it is probably still the most advanced country in the world. With a vengeance, Japan has formidable powers of economic expansion, out-

From the Tokyo
Metropolitan Government
Building

standing capabilities in organization, work, investment and research, and, above all, a sense of accuracy and precision in the production of manufactured goods. This adds a contemporary perspective to an ancient tradition, where well-made things are considered more valuable than the rarity or age of the objects themselves. Next, there is the urban landscape, and the way it builds up through superimposition and stratification, with highways spreading over two or three levels, small wooden houses and magnificent, flawless skyscrapers, all on a land subdivision that appears medieval to our eyes; the cityscape achieves whirling density in its omnivorous imitative power, thus verifying its structural development."[4] Such insight is certainly not isolated. In fact, in the last few years, town planners and architects have been focusing on Tokyo, which is by now a privileged subject, with exceptional critical interest. This has led to such a wealth of specialized literature that it has become known as "Tōkyōron," or "Tokyology." This is hardly a coincidence.

But what is more important is that underlying such apparently abstract debate, Tokyo poses a great problem: does it represent the final degeneration of the Western city, as we can easily be led to think from our own viewpoint? Or is it something totally different? Has its long, continuous historical diversity enabled it to maintain a distinct cultural in-

15

Night view

From the Tokyo
Metropolitan Government
Building

Night view

Shinjuku

dependence that has remained significantly unmodified despite its recent, intense hybridization with the West? Furthermore, is this why we are so interested in it? Or, since the city (the term itself, as already noted, reveals obvious inadequacies) is not a part of Western tradition, has it—or does it appear to have—taken up an age-long challenge no other city has ever ventured? Has it launched itself forwards with vertiginous, lightning-fast transformations in its architectural, urban and, more generally, cultural landscape, with the energy, recklessness and aggressiveness that only those who have never played a historical role in Western tradition can achieve? In other words, is Tokyo the ultimate result of Western urban culture, or has it independently developed from a line that has continued, unbroken, since the ancient times of Edo (as it was called until 1868)? Given its overtaking of the great Western metropolises, might the 1970s reappraisal of Japanese culture (which, of course, also has a name: nihonjinron, "nipponology" or, better yet, "essays on Japanese uniqueness") involve rewriting the city's history? In the early 1990s Augustin Berque wrote: "What is here at stake is of global concern. In the present world situation—that of a Japanese supremacy in the production of riches, which had ensured Western hegemony—the point is whether Japan will oust the West from its hegemonic position. This question entails the following: hegemonies in the past, from Babylon to New York, having always been embodied by the townscape of an emblematic city, will the forms of Tokyo embody this symbolic reversal?"[5]

To some extent, our perception of Tokyo today has changed since the years Berque wrote these words. The slowdown in Japanese economy, the

Electric Town, Akihabara

growth of the European Union and the undisputed leadership of America have certainly cooled expectations (and fears) that the city would rush way out front, thus enabling observers to form much more detached and mature opinions. But, possibly, it is this very detachment that induces us to reflect yet again on the role that Tokyo is currently playing on the global scene, leading us to consider that, perhaps more than any other city in the world, it does indeed seem to be substantiating a new symbolic form within the urban phenomena of the 21st century.

Geography

It is common knowledge that Tokyo, which occupies the extensive Kantō alluvial plain, lies on Honshū, the largest and by far the most densely populated island of the Japanese archipelago. The city is situated on the eastern coast, where most of the country's population is concentrated, and is set around a wide, sheltered bay of relatively shallow water that opens southwards toward the Pacific Ocean.

Numerous water courses cut through its territory, which is set on low hills; its main river is the Sumida, the same name as the last tract of the Arakawa range. This gently undulating landscape is closed off in the distance by a mountain range that is dominated by the soaring Fuji volcano toward the southeast. Counting both the rivers and canals, still today Tokyo has 2,155 kilometers of water courses crossed by almost 6,000 bridges; in fact, water is perhaps the city's only real, plentiful natural resource, on which its wealth and ancient settling culture were based.

Scale model of Tokyo, Mori
Building Corporation

Its latitude is more or less the same as that of Tangiers, the Mediterranean islands of Crete and Pantelleria, and southern California, between San Francisco and Los Angeles. It is the easternmost of all the great Asian cities, but at the same time it is an extreme outpost of the continent; it is giddily perched over the ocean deeps (just to the east, the water plunges to depths of over 10,000 meters) at the extreme northwest point of the Pacific Rim—the volcanic and highly seismic, almost uninterrupted strip of land that emerges all around this immense ocean. This explains Tokyo's high geological instability, the highest on the planet.

Tokyo is the Pacific area's undisputed leader. It is mainly Korea and China that look to Japan, as, from a historical viewpoint, the latter has interacted—more or less conflictually—for centuries with these two countries. Japan has creatively inherited its script and literature from these nations, as well as Buddhism and Confucianism. Australia, New Zealand and the North American West Coast, from Seattle to Los Angeles, are also directing their attention toward Japan.

Shibuya

Shinjuku

A canal in Bunkyō-ku

The Tokyo Metropolitan
Expressway in Nihonbashi

The Tokyo Metropolitan
Expressway

The Kanagawa River
in Akihabara

The Tokyo Metropolitan
Expressway in Nihonbashi

Viaduct over the Arakawa
River

Buildings on Meguro-dōri,
Minato-ku

Wangan-dōri near the Fuji
Building, Teleport Town

Wangan-dōri,
Teleport Town

Shuto Expressway
in Roppongi

Houses in Iidabashi

Shibuya

Solar panel towers

Mariko Mori, *Red Light*, 1994

The City Image

Tokyo offers such an impressive urban spectacle that even from a visual point of view it may constitute the world's most staggering cityscape. Viewed from Rainbow Bridge, the long, dizzily high bridge over the bay; from the overhead highway strips "that transform traveling across the city into a roller coaster ride";[6] from Tokyo Tower, a late 1950s copy of the Eiffel Tower that is slightly higher than the original; or from the imposing City Hall towers, which house the city government, the city extends as far as the eye can see and is in ceaseless motion across its entire, boundless vastness. You can "feel" its noise, its power, its infinite vitality. It is overwhelming, fascinating, hypnotizing.

The figures are impressive, too. There are 15 million inhabitants, all within one administratively independent prefecture, Tokyo-to, which is split up into 23 "ku," or wards, covering 598 square kilometers. The system is run by the Tokyo Metropolitan Government. Its three central wards—Chiyoda, Chuo and Minato—form the Central Business District (CBD) where, as well as extensive residential and tourist areas, there is the largest concentration of government buildings, offices belonging to Japanese and foreign companies, banks, embassies and so on. Since 1991, however, the Tokyo Metropolitan Government has operated from Shinjuku, in line with a decentralizing plan for the development of civic centers in six of the 23 wards: Shinjuku itself, Shibuya, Ikebukuro, Ueno/Asakusa, Kinshichō/Kameido and Osaki. Shinjuku in particular seems to be establishing itself as Tokyo's new

View of Shibuya-ku from the Tokyo Metropolitan Government Building

downtown. In addition, the Tama district must be included, with over 3.5 million inhabitants on a 1,160-square-kilometer area, as well as the bay islands—some of which are very far from the city—comprising 30,000 inhabitants over 400 square kilometers.

But, in reality, if daily commuting patterns are added to the equation, the Japanese capital's metropolitan area is made up of an even more extensive conurbation. Commuters fan out over distances of over 150 kilometers, coming from an additional three "ken" (prefectures): Kanagawa to the southwest, which includes the Yokohama metropolis; Saitama to the north; and Chiba to the southeast. Taken together, they form an administrative entity known as the Tokyo Metropolitan Region. With over 30 million inhabitants, the geographical area of the Kantō plain is home to 25% of the country's population, a third of its professionals, technicians, managers and skilled workers, as well as 36.2% of its factories. In comparison, Kansai, Japan's second most developed area, dominated by Osaka and comprising Kyōto, Nara and Kōbe in addition to a series of minor centers, varies between 15% and 23% and, notably, has 14.5% of its workers in the production sector against Kantō's 28%.[7]

The National Capital Region is even more extensive; it is such a vast administrative entity that it is hardly able to function as a recognizable economic unit. Although it is obviously dominated by Tokyo, it contains a series of lesser centers from much farther afield, belonging to various prefectures, such as Ibaraki. Taken as a whole, it is one of the world's most

Rainbow Bridge

Overleaf
Rainbow Bridge
from Teleport Town

Tachū Naitō and Nikken
Sekkei, Tokyo Tower, Shiba
Koen, Minato-ku, 1958

Chuo-dōri in Ginza

Overleaf
Minato-ku

extensive and most highly populated urban areas, and forms a diversified, complex, continuous polycentric system that has gradually absorbed a series of cities which were formerly separate entities.[8]

More than any other megalopolis, Tokyo seems to be the very embodiment of the contradictions of contemporary urban culture. The amount of private space per capita is 66% lower than in New York; an average apartment is no larger than 55 square meters, compared with 85 square meters in Rome or Singapore and 90 square meters in Paris; parks only take up 5% of the land surface as opposed to 30% in London; despite the highly efficient metropolitan railroad system, three out of four workers travel over an hour daily; over 70% get less than six hours' sleep; 41% of married couples cannot speak to each other for more than 15 minutes a day— and this includes a 10% who have no chance of doing so at all.[9] The cost of living is 50% higher than in New York; at the end of 2000, estimates set it as the world's highest. The rebuilding rate is very high, as well: a building's average life is 26 years, against 44 in the United States and 75 in the United Kingdom. With subtle understatement, Fumihiko Maki once said: "I wonder whether we are wasting our resources in paying attention to the life-span of a building we are constructing."[10] And yet, despite the high densities, the amount of space that is actually used within the huge dimensions of the 23 "ku" is only 52% of the total (although this reaches 70% in the central areas); this gives some idea of the high development potential that still remains.

Yet, this system has reached incredible levels of productivity, efficiency, creativity, cleanliness and safety, with one of the world's most advanced and powerful concentrations of economy, technology and culture. Despite the many recent signs of crisis, the quality of life is still surprisingly high. It is a system that seems to answer Bernard Tschumi's appeal for a "post-humanistic [city], which is able to play a part in a time where notions of unity and consistency no longer directly apply, . . . characterized by what might be called decentralization, a dispersion of the subject."[11] A system that actually seems to put the future on stage, where we cannot but think that, after all, "chaos" is no more than "an order to be deciphered."[12]

[1] Quoted in F. Maraini, *Ore Giapponesi*. Milan: Corbaccio, 2000, p. 60.
[2] C. Brandi, *Budda sorride*. Turin: Einaudi, 1973. Quoted in F. Maraini.
[3] A. Berque. "La città giapponese. Uso di un'immagine," in *Casabella*, no. 608-609, 1994.
[4] V. Gregotti, "Una modernità dis-orientata," in *Casabella*, no. 608-609, 1994.
[5] A. Berque.
[6] M. Biraghi, "La città come pratica rituale," in *Casabella*, no. 669, 1999.
[7] See S. Sassen, *The Global City, New York, London, Tokyo*. Princeton: Princeton University Press, 1991, p. 213.
[8] See S. Sassen, pp. 343-344.
[9] See M. Mori, H. Yamagata, B. Mau, *New Tokyo Life Style Think Zone*. Tokyo: Minoru Mori, 2001.
[10] See *Saper credere in architettura, trentadue domande a Fumihiko Maki*, edited by L. Spita. Naples: Clean, 2003, p. 31.
[11] B. Tschumi, "La ville éclatée," in *Ville forme symbolique projet*. Brussels: IFA, 1986, p. 98.
[12] J. Saramago, *L'uomo duplicato*. Turin: Einaudi, 2003, p. 88. Or. ed. *O Homen Duplicado*. Lisbon 2002.

Nishi-Shinjuku

Yokohama

Yokohama Bay

Yokohama from the Port
Terminal

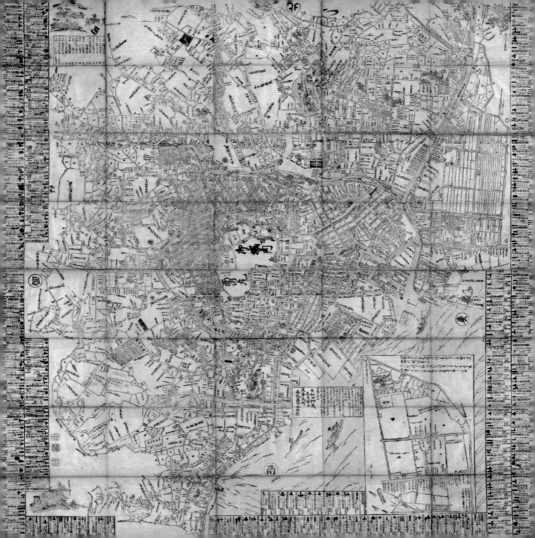

2. History

Japan, it's name meaning "at the roots of the sun," has ancient origins. At the end of the 1800s, a series of prehistoric settlements came to light in the region of Kantō. In Tokyo itself, the most ancient archeological remains are in the area of Ōi, in Shinagawa.

Despite traditional theories that postulated their divine origins, its inhabitants, the "Sun children", resulted from population flows from the southern Pacific and from the northern region of the Asian continent. The latter, and maybe the former as well, made use of the "bridge" formed by the Korean Peninsula.

Ancient documents prove that relations with China date back to the 1st century B.C. The first Westerner to mention the country was Marco Polo. He called it "Zipagu" and reported that, "the peoples are white," adding, prophetically, that "this island's wealth is incalculable."

The country's history reveals different periods of tension, and is punctuated by alternating stages of "openness" and "closure" to foreigners: in the 6th and 7th centuries A.D. it opened up to Buddhism and Chinese culture; in the 15th and 16th centuries to the Europeans; finally, in the second half of the 1800s, to the West and the rest of the world.

The Edo Period

Tokyo took on its current name, meaning "Capital of the East," on September 13th 1868, at the time the Meiji dynasty was restored. This marked the inauguration of a new era in which the country came to modernity—and not only symbolically.

The city—which, as aforementioned, was called Edo, meaning "estuary"—was probably founded as a fortified settlement in 1457 by Ōta Dōkan (1432-86), a minor feudal lord from a cadet branch of the Uesugi family. However, the primitive fortress soon passed into the hands of the Hōjō dynasty from Odawara. The city's military origins seem to have marked its history from the beginning; even today, Tokyo is striking for its power and hardness, in contrast to more ancient, aristocratic, spiritual and refined cities such as Kyōto and Nara.

The Portuguese, whose trading bases in the Orient were mainly constituted by Goa and Macao, formed contacts with the Japanese in the middle of the 16th century ("arigatò," one of the ways of saying "thank you" in Japan, is none other than a corruption of the Portuguese "obrigado"). In 1549, St. Francis Xavier landed in Japan and founded the first Jesuit mission. Evangelism immediately brought good results: between the end of the 1500s and the early 1600s, nearly half a million people were christened.

Hyoshiya Ichirobe, 1684

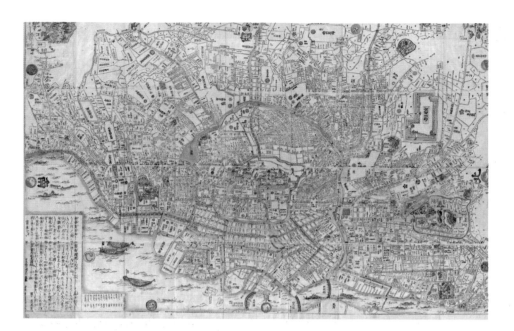

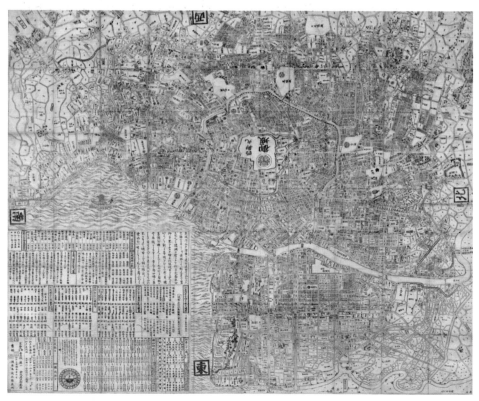

Ishikawa and Ryusen,
Bundo Edo oezu, 1710

Kanamaru, Hikogoro,
Subaraya and Mohe,
Bunken Edo oezu, 1803

Overleaf
Map of Edo/Tokyo
1844-1848

In 1590, the "warlord" Tokugawa Ieyasu settled in Edo, concentrating a dictatorial military power there. He assumed the title of Shōgun, possibly in more or less open opposition to the emperor, and his dynasty retained its power for many years. Ieyasu suspected that apparently innocuous religious conversions might actually be concealing political revolt, so he instigated "sakoku," an exclusion policy against all Europeans, who were known as the "namban-jin," or "barbarians of the south." This would be continued by his successors for almost three centuries. The imperial court remained in Kyōto, the ancient capital which had been founded in 794, but the country's political center shifted northwards.

1603 saw the construction of the Nihonbashi bridge. Its wooden structure, 50 meters long, marked the forking of the five great roads controlled by the shōgun administration: Tōkaidō, Nakasendō, Koshū Kaidō, Nikko Kaidō and Ōshū Kaidō. Hence, Nihonbashi formed a sort of convergence point for trade, and even today the bridge is still regarded as such.

A new castle was built between 1604 and 1619. The Daimyō—feudal lords who divided their time between the city and the provinces while their families were held more or less hostage in the capital—had to contribute to its construction; one of their number, Tōdō Takatora (1556-1630), an expert architect, was entrusted with overseeing the project. Three rings of concentric walls defended the castle from external attack. A fairly distinct urban structure had already been achieved: the areas of greatest prestige—Yamanote, or the High City—spread to the west; those housing the lower classes, including artisans and merchants, were to the east, in Shitamachi, the Low City—on marshy lands subject to the bay's rising tides and river floods.

The first Spanish ship reached Japan in 1615. It had been sent by Philip III and came from the Mexican port of Acapulco. In the same year, a Japanese delegation left the northern city of Sendai to meet Pope Paul V Borghese in Rome. In other words, a new period of relations with the West appeared to be dawning. But in 1616, the xenophobe Hidetada, a proud enemy of Christianity, became Shōgun. For nearly 20 years, Christians were persecuted relentlessly; during the Shimabara revolt, only 105 of the 37,000 peasants who had been converted to Christianity escaped death.

Aside from a tiny Dutch settlement in Nagasaki which was indirectly connected with Europe by a ship that arrived from Macao once a year, the archipelago was closed to all outside influence. This isolation was to last almost two and a half centuries and had a deep effect on the culture of the city and the entire nation. Seclusion did not hinder the country's development, but it doubtlessly fostered independence and diversity, thus marking its character indelibly.

By roughly 1640, the Edo castle had become the largest in Japan, and possibly the world. The imposing central structure was laid out on five floors, covering an extensive area where Higashi Gyoen, the "East Garden," now lies, northeast of today's Imperial Palace. The external ring of walls (gaikaku), marked by a 50-meter-wide moat, ran for 16 kilometers. The inner walls (naikaku) had 11 gates, the main one being Omotemon.

Immediately afterwards, in 1657, Edo was devastated by what is known as the great fire of Meireki. Over 100,000 people died, and 60% of its buildings went up in smoke, including 350 temples and sanctuaries. It was one of the greatest catastrophes in Edo's history, but certainly not the only one; as we shall see, throughout history the city has suffered a continuous succession of destructive events, followed by reconstruction. This explains its continuously "young" appearance despite its ancient origins. It also explains its nature, which, while accepting instability and physical renewal on one side, is still firmly attached to tradition on the other.

The castle, too, suffered serious damage; rebuilding began almost immediately (the Fujimi tower, one of the three still in existence, dates from 1659, for example), but the old defensive system of walls and moats was no longer considered in line with the times, and at a certain point development work was stopped. Nevertheless, the size and grandeur that this ancient structure had attained by the middle of the 17th century was destined to remain unsurpassed.

More generally, urban reconstruction was characterized by measures meant to prevent further disasters. Density was drastically reduced and a firm policy of expansion across the territory was adopted: by around 1670, the city already covered an area of 63 square kilometers. In the first years

of the 19th century, the population reached 800,000, making Edo the largest city in the world (according to the 1820 census, New York, for instance, had 123,706 inhabitants at that time). By the middle of that century it had exceeded one million. The city was soon provided with an advanced system of 175 canals, 84 of which were navigable, and other waterworks to prevent continuous flooding. Shitamachi's population density continued to remain very high, reaching 70,000 inhabitants per square meter, and its road structure, protected by closed barriers, was already labyrinthine.

It was only in 1853 that the Japanese finally emerged from isolation, namely, two years after the publication of Melville's aforementioned novel. Four American military vessels, the famous "black ships" commanded by Commodore M.C. Perry, set anchor threateningly in the bay of Edo and practically forced the country to embark on a new period of trade. The first American-Japanese treaty was drawn up in 1854. In comparison, Chinese ports had already been open to foreign trade since 1685.

In 1858, Yokohama, which at that time was no more than a village of 300 inhabitants spread out on the Ōka river delta, became one of the four ports indicated in the treaty. The first railroad line in Japan linked it to Tokyo in 1872; it was only 30 kilometers long and was built by a British company. Yokohama thus began to grow rapidly, becoming a highly desirable destination for foreigners settling in Japan, as well as a naval port; in 1889 it had 120,000 inhabitants, and by 1930 this figure had grown to 600,000. Today it still has the highest concentration of foreign citizens, especially Chinese and Koreans.

The Meiji Restoration and the march toward modernity
In 1868, Shōgun Tokugawa Keiki abdicated, the military shogunate was abolished and the Meiji dynasty—the "Illuminated Government"—was restored under Emperor Mutsuhito. In spite of uncertainties, controversies and political difficulties, Edo became the new capital of the whole country, and its name was changed to Tokyo. After over a thousand years of rule in Kyōto, the Court and the entire imperial administration were transferred to a very large city; their new home already extended over almost 80 square kilometers.

The Meiji Restoration was a highly significant, unprecedented phenomenon. In addition to unifying the Empire and eliminating the anomaly of the shogunate, it initiated a revolutionary period of openness to the West which started precisely with the "refoundation" of its new capital. A millennial culture (architecture included) therefore suddenly found itself exposed to European novelties. Forced to reexamine themselves and their ancient, immutable traditions, the Japanese in general, and Tokyo in particular started their controversial but relentless, amazing and giddy march toward modernity.

A great number of highly radical changes were made. A constitution was framed on the French model in 1869; in 1872 education became compulsory, and the Gregorian calendar was introduced. This was substitute for the traditional one, which originated in China; it is divided into 12 months that follow the lunar cycles, and the years are counted according to each Emperor's investiture. This old system still prevails today. In 1870, the Ministry of Engineering saw the establishment of a building division. As a result, a number of foreign technicians were invited to Tokyo, including the Italian C.V. Cappelletti (who designed the History Museum and the headquarters for staff officers), the American R.P. Bridgens and the Frenchman C. de Boinville. Shortly afterwards, in 1875, the first course of architecture was introduced at the Faculty of Engineering. Military service became obligatory in 1873. Clashes between the regular army and the samurai were very violent. On October 24th 1877 a group of samurai rebelled and, armed only with swords and halberds, desperately attempted a coup d'état. Almost all of them were killed, and the few survivors committed suicide according to the "seppuku" ritual. These events thus marked the fall of the ancient warrior caste.

In 1880, freedom of worship was introduced along with Sunday rest, a modern penal code and a new constitution based on the Prussian model; a new civil code followed in 1898.

Meanwhile, in 1872, another fire had destroyed the central districts of Ginza and Tsukiji; the latter, especially, had a high percentage of foreign residents. From then on, buildings were to be built with fireproof materials, and the traditional wood was abandoned—Ginza took on the name of "Rengagai" or "Bricktown." Reconstruction was supervised by Thomas J. Waters, an Englishman who had arrived in Japan during the last shōgun's government, and who had designed the mint in Ōsaka. Little was known of Waters before his arrival from Europe; he left Japan in 1877 and disappeared without trace.

The newly triggered process of westernization continued with the creation of a new social center, a real meeting point for Japanese and Europeans. It was in Rokumeikan, not far from where the famous Imperial Hotel was due to rise, and was designed by another Englishman, Josiah Conder. In 1886, a new executive center was built near the Imperial Palace. The

V. Van Gogh, *Japonaiserie: Oiran*, 1887
Van Gogh Museum, Amsterdam

Trading ships in the port of Tsukuda

The Shibusawa villa in Kabuto-chō

Minister Kaoru Inoue, who was probably impressed by the German architectural and urban achievements under Bismarck, invited two architects from Berlin, Hermann Ende and Wilhelm Böckmann, to shape a plan for the new hub. A first ambitious, magniloquent plan, featuring great radiating avenues with high-sounding names (Mikado, Empress, Japan etc.) was followed by a more streamlined proposal made only by Ende for the area around Hibiya Park. In the end, after the two architects had made detailed plans for a great number of buildings, only two were built: the Ministry of Justice and the Supreme Court. For the occasion, twenty Japanese, including architects, carpenters, plasterers and so on, were sent to Germany to train as technical apprentices. The Ministry of Justice is a particularly unusual, imposing example of German Neo-Renaissance architecture, a variant of the style known as Second Empire, and is practically one of a kind, since the German originals in the style were destroyed during World War II. Like other similar buildings, its presence in the setting of the contemporary metropolis is as dignified as it is ambiguous, as if it were a surviving witness to the 19th-century clash between European cultural imperialism and an ancient Japanese civilization that was unprepared for novelty.

The Tokyo City Improvement Ordinance was issued in 1888, a first attempt at a modern establishment for urban planning in the new capital. This was aimed at improving the road and rail networks, ensuring efficient water resources, and making the rivers, parks, bridges, markets,

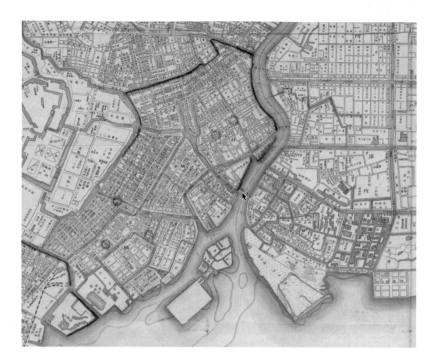

Kanazawa and Ryota,
Shinsen Tokyo zenzu, 1892

cemeteries and gardens more viable. Still today, the city's target is to come up to Western standards, and for over a century, this has been the spur for policies related to public works. It was in this context that the go-ahead for the new railroad link between Shimbashi and Ueno was given in 1890. The first, experimental steel building was built in 1895, the year Japan won the war with China and annexed Formosa. This revealed the first signs of a disquieting growth in Nipponese expansionistic ambitions.

The second half of the 19th century also revealed that Japanese architecture and art were objects of renewed interest for Western scholars. For instance, impressionist painters were deeply affected by the art of "ukiyo-e," the so-called "floating world." This term developed from its original Buddhist philosophical stance, which alluded to the transcience of worldly things, until it embraced the prints and paintings of worldly subjects that were in great demand throughout the whole Edo period. If Henry Cole and Owen Jones were already inspired by the Far East in their publications, Walter Crane came under its influence between 1859 and 1862, while working as an engraver for William James Linton. Moreover, Japanese prints were already circulating in Paris in 1856, and shops selling Japanese *objets d'art* and furnishings were opening both in Paris and London. Many avant-garde artists collected prints by Hiroshige and Utamaro; Manet, Monet and Degas often drew inspiration from them for their works; in 1887 Van Gogh painted "The Courtesan," now at the Van Gogh Museum in Amsterdam, which reproduces a kimono-clad figure by Kesai Eisen.

In 1886, the American E.S. Morse published the first book on Japanese architecture, *Japanese Homes and Their Surroundings*, followed in 1889 by the German, J. Brinkmann, with his handbook *Kunst und Handwerk in Japan*. These are works that look at the more picturesque aspects of this exotic culture, but which nevertheless had a significant influence on Art Nouveau taste, especially through representations of the natural world.

The First Decades of the 20ᵗʰ Century

The opening of the 20ᵗʰ century coincided with a further strong drive toward westernization. By then, Tokyo had become a prefecture, with a population of 2.4 million in 1905.

This is the year in which a young, enterprising American architect, Frank Lloyd Wright, first set foot in Tokyo. As we shall see further on, he was only to have a relative influence on the Japanese architectural scene. Yet, his arrival seems to have marked the beginning of a period in which America's presence became stronger and stronger, and more and more significant, to a point where—most notably in the second half of the 20ᵗʰ century—the city's image was so transformed that it looked quite similar to an American metropolis.

Those were years of great military expansionism, as well. Between 1904 and 1905 Japan waged, and won, a war against the Russian Tsar's empire, extending its territories to halfway across the island of Sakhalin; in 1910 it annexed Korea.

49

Just a few years earlier, in 1906, plans for the Tokyo Station had begun. Facing the new Marunouchi business quarter, near the Imperial Palace, it was to give the city a great central station and connect the various lines that already existed. The works, entrusted to Kingo Tatsuno and Manji Kasai, began in 1908 and were completed in 1914. The steel structure (steel was imported from Great Britain and the United States) was discerningly faced with local bricks. The procedure was typical of the Beaux Arts taste and reinforced the image of Ginza's Bricktown and other neighboring areas of the time. The overall appearance of the building recalls Amsterdam's Central Station, and it might even have been directly influenced by it. The station survived the 1923 earthquake, but was partially destroyed during World War II; with the exception of two large cupolas, it was then carefully rebuilt.

In 1912, an office building belonging to an insurance company was the first to feature reinforced concrete. Shortly afterwards, in 1914, the Taishō Exhibition in Ueno was inaugurated. Many of the pavilions clearly revealed influences from the latest European Architectural trends: Art Nouveau and especially Viennese Secession. But four years earlier, construction of the second National Diet Building (the first was destroyed in a fire in 1890, two months after its inauguration) had begun, witnessing what confusion the best architectural culture of the time was wreaking on Tokyo. This building, which was to house the parliament, was an ambiguous structure modeled on the Mausoleum of Halikarnossos, one of the ancient world's seven wonders.

Pertinently, in 1910 the Architectural Institute of Japan organized a debate on the theme, "What should the country's future architectural style be like?" Similar deliberations had been going on for almost a cen-

Kobayashi and Gisaburo, *Tokyo shigai chizu*, 1904

Ando and Rikinosuke, *Tokyo shi-zenzu*, 1905

tury across the whole Western world. In 1828, for instance, a text by Heinrich Hübsch appeared; it was entitled *Im Welchem Style Sollen Wir Bauen?* ("In Which Style Should We Build?") But in Japan, the renewed controversy took on new connotations. It was no longer simply a debate between conservatives and innovators, but rather between those who—like Yashukura Ohtsuka—believed that opening up to the West was indispensable, albeit its messages were to be adapted to native contexts and methods; and those who, like Chinto Itoh, tried to defend national architectural culture, inviting architects to "purify" their ideas by immersing them in the waters of ancient traditions. At one point, the Bunriha secessionist group came into the debate: it was against any form of historicism and was supported by Wright and by the Nihon Kōsaku Bunka Remmei, the Japanese Association for Industrial Design, which leaned toward rationalism tempered by an inclination to restore tradition. Obviously, no clear answers emerged. What did emerge, though, was the double dissatisfaction that came from the pursuit of European styles (an obviously naive practice) on one side, and the waning possibility of restoring past traditions on the other—due mainly to the inadequacy of the materials and building techniques. Benevolo points out the extent of the crisis concisely: "In these terms, any profitable relationship between European architectural philosophy and Japanese tradition is impossible; imitating European models has not only supplanted local tradition, but has disintegrated it, rendering it virtually useless, as it has been dismembered into a multitude of abstract components."[1]

In spite of all this, when Emperor Mutsuhito died in 1912, the capital was already a fairly modern city, if seen from a Western viewpoint. The projects run by the Tokyo City Improvement Ordinance went on until 1918. In 1919, at the end of World War I, the enactment of the City Planning Law constituted the first systematic approach to the difficulties of planning in the contemporary metropolis. In addition to making extensive use of zoning regulations, the law also attempted to promote the regrouping of small, anachronistic land parcels through a set of rules modeled on the German "Lex Adickes." Meanwhile, the population kept on increasing inexorably, stimulated by massive internal migration and the industrialization sparked off by the end of the hostilities. This led to great difficulties in managing the city. The Tokyo prefecture had practically doubled its population in little more than two decades, and in 1920 it reached 3.7 million.

The Great Earthquake of Kantō

In the 1900s, Tokyo was hit by two highly destructive events: an earthquake and World War II. The former dates back to 1923 and became known as "Kantō-daijishin," "The Great Earthquake of Kantō." On September 1st, precisely at noon, the city was shaken by a violet seism. However, it was not so much the earthquake itself that caused the greatest damage as its indirect effects. Almost all of the buildings were still in wood, and over 50% of them were destroyed by the fires, set off by the seism, which spread everywhere, fed by strong winds. There were 142,807 casu-

alties—which exceeded the number who had perished during the great Meireki fire of 1657—and most of them met a horrible death, as they were burned alive.

The reconstruction work that followed during the 1920s and 1930s included an ambitious plan for residential building financed by the government. It comprised a series of 16 experimental settlements meant for the middle classes, built between 1925 and 1927 in Tokyo and Yokohama, and known as "Dōjunkai" ("Mutual Profit Association"). The three-story houses were of the traditional type—bathrooms were shared—set around functional courtyards, and were built in reinforced concrete. They were met with great success, and the ones that have survived to this day are still in demand. The Aoyama Apartments in Shibuya are the most notable and successful example of this kind of planning. After the war, they were sold to their tenants. A great number of them have now been turned into small offices, showrooms and boutiques, complying with the predictably strong commercial pressures in an area that skirts the elegant tree-lined avenue of Omotesando.

Kotaro Sakurai's Marunouchi was built in 1926. This huge office building, which included a number of retail stores, was designed by the Fuller company of New York. With over 10,000 square meters on each of its eight floors, it remained the largest building in Japan for over 40 years.

The 1930s saw the introduction of the Modern Movement by a handful of innovators who had confronted and measured themselves against the Europeans. In 1934, Bunzo Yamaguchi designed the attractive Orthodontics school; Tetsuro Yoshida created a series of interesting buildings marked by sober functionalism—one of the most notable examples of this is the central Post Office headquarters (1931) in Maronouchi, not far from Tokyo Station. Yoshida also authored a book, *Das japanische Wohnhaus*, which was published in German in 1935. Another exponent of the movement was Junzo Sakakura, who together with José Luís Sert and Alvar Aalto won the Grand Prix at the Paris World Exhibition of 1937, for which he designed the Japanese pavilion. Sakakura was work-

View of the Hie temple in the early 20th century

Overleaf
A bird's-eye view of Greater Tokyo, 1921

ing with Le Corbusier at the time. Other innovators were Sutemi Horiguchi, the architect who created the experimental Wasaka house in 1939; Kunio Maekawa, who had worked at Le Corbusier's studio between 1928 and 1930; and Togo Murano. The latter in particular was to have a leading role in the delicate architectural mediation between the old and new. After beginning his career with Setsu Watanabe, Murano opened his own studio in 1929, and two years later he completed his first independently designed building. This was the Morigo Building in Nihonbashi-Muromachi, which then became the Kinsan Building: an essential, austere seven-story block in reinforced concrete, completely faced in brown brickwork, with finely proportioned rectangular windows. Bruno Taut hailed it as a masterpiece.

In 1938, the year Kenzō Tange graduated with a sober plan for a Fine Arts Palace, Jin Watanabe and Yosaku Matsumoto presented a project for an insurance company, the Dai'chi Mutual Life offices, which was one of the last important buildings to be planned with the onset of war; indeed, works were interrupted by the conflict. Before being completed, it was taken over by the American troops for their headquarters; still today, General MacArthur's office has been kept as it was. The building was radically renovated by Kevin Roche in the early 1990s, but the original façade has remained intact.

World War II

Following a pact stipulated in 1940, the Japanese joined the war as German and Italian allies, although they were not physically at their side. Japan had withdrawn from the League of Nations in 1938; throughout a period marked by sinister, autocratic nationalism, the country successfully carried out a long series of harsh expansionist military actions in China and Southeast Asia.

In 1941, during a feverish moment following a relatively long period of United States neutrality, the American Ambassador in Tokyo, Joseph C. Grew, seriously warned President Roosevelt of the imminent possibil-

55

ity of attack. In Japan, a climate of collective self-exaltation probably prevented the high military hierarchies from making any reliable evaluation of America's true strength. This may have been what underlay a plan that was sheer folly, conceived and set in motion by Isoroku Yamamoto, the Admiral and Vice Minister of the Navy: to destroy the United States presence in the Pacific.[2] On December 7th 1941, the Japanese Airforce made a surprise attack on the United States naval base of Pearl Harbor, in the Hawaiian Islands.

The day after, the United States declared war. But there was a long wait before the onset of military action: the first bombardment did not hit the Japanese capital until April 1942. In the meantime, Japan had successfully invaded the Philippines, Hong Kong, Kuala Lumpur, Singapore, Java and Burma. But soon it was all over. A crescendo of air raids went on over the next three years, especially during 1944 through to March 1945.

"The bombardment of March 9th-10th, for example, started around 10:30 pm and went on all night: several hundred B-29s (now they look like toys, but at that time they were the most powerful bombers in the world) rained down thousands of tons of fragmentation and incendiary bombs on the lower-class quarters of the city. The fire, boosted by a tempestuous wind, blazed infernally. The day after the bombing, what had been the most populous part of Tokyo, a dense mass of houses, workshops, warehouses, public buildings and light industrial plants, was just a ravaged, charred, smoking plain."[3]

Bombardments continued until August; Tokyo suffered 70 air raids in all. On August 6th 1945, Hiroshima was struck by an atomic bomb; three days later it was Nagasaki's turn. Annihilated, the country was forced to surrender.

In his unpublished autobiography, Arata Isozaki reports: "That August 15th 1945, the day Japan surrendered, the sky was a cloudless blue over the archipelago. I was a 15-year-old boy then, and even I felt that an epoch was coming to an end, but I had no idea of what might be about to begin. All I knew was that the noise had stopped. And for a moment there was no sound at all. . . . Throughout my youth, until I began studying architecture, I had constantly found myself facing destruction, as well as the elimination of the tangible things that surrounded me."[4]

Shortly earlier, Fosco Maraini, who had been held in custody along with other Italians—as they were all suspected of anti-fascism—had been evacuated with his family to Kōsai-ji and moved to a temple not far from Koromo (now Toyota City). He recorded: "On the fifteenth of the month, a young boy hurried over to tell us that the Emperor was going to speak on the radio: it was the first time in history that such a thing had happened and everyone was astounded. 'Perhaps he is going to tell us that we have to fight to death', suggested one of the policemen weakly: but you could tell he was just saying that to save face. Then something really odd happened. The Emperor made his speech (in which he actually did announce the surrender), but none of the Japanese around us could understand him. The text was, in fact, in a language that was only known at court—it was so different from everyday speech that you had to be a philologist to make sense of it."[5]

Hirohito, the "King of the Sky," had done something that had never happened during the country's very ancient history: he had addressed his subjects directly, announcing, more or less, that events were not going according to his wishes. But the listening Japanese were more stunned about hearing the voice of the divinity than by the dramatic—and obscure—content of his speech.

The defeat marked the end of a world. Throughout its agelong history, Japan had never been successfully invaded by any foreign enemy, not even by Kublai Khan, and its army had never been beaten. This led to a large number of suicides, as many as 50 in front of the Imperial Palace alone. However, the majority adapted to the course of events, assuming a passive attitude.

Although Tokyo did not suffer directly from the nuclear devastation of Hiroshima and Nagasaki, it emerged from the war as it would have from a catastrophe. In February 1944, the population was 7.3 million; just 21 months later, in November 1945, it had dropped to 3.5 million, and everyone was weak from hunger. A quarter of a million had died. A fourth of the city had been razed to the ground. Half the houses, the ancient Meiji-jingū and Sensō-ji temples, as well as the Edo castle, had been destroyed. All along an extended stretch of downtown Tokyo, from Hibiya to Shinjuku—eight kilometers—nothing was left standing.

The Postwar Years

The country was occupied by the Allies, mainly the Americans, from 1945 to 1952; these seven years saw a long process of demilitarization and forced democratization. The armed forces were dismantled; colonies were lost; those who were responsible for dreadful war crimes were tried by special courts; the old governing political and economic class lost all its power.

The Emperor was forced to renounce his divine status: during his New Year speech in 1946, with the so-called "declaration of humanity," he disavowed his descent from the Sun Goddess Amaterasu, thus disclaiming any kind of divine attribute. In 1947, a new constitution was drawn up, basically, by the Supreme Command of the Allied Forces, and the Emperor was reduced to no more than a state symbol. The state itself was separated from the official Shintō religion. The nobility was abolished. Women were finally allowed to vote. A system of parliamentary government based on the British system was set up. The country was obliged to abjure war expressly, except in the eventuality of self-defense, and furthermore, a land reform was drawn up, which redistributed the land itself and emancipated it from a feudal theocratic system that had lasted, unchanged, for several thousand years.

After a long period in which it appeared that Tokyo could not hope to recover, little by little the 1950s saw a new, overwhelming population increase and the beginnings of an even more overwhelming economic growth. In 1951, Japan signed the San Francisco peace treaty, reestablishing relations with the United States. On their part, the Americans saw the country as a strong bulwark against the expansion of communism in Asia, and thus enthusiastically embarked on a major investment plan. Many new corporations set up their offices in the capital, abandoning Ōsaka despite its historic trading primacy.

Redevelopment was entrusted to a governmental agency; the emergency and the need for new housing led the agency to place quantity over quality. This was the time when a new system of support for public housing was devised: the Public Operated Housing (POH) rented homes that were financed and managed by local governments; the Housing and Urban Development Corporation (HUDC)—which, from 1955 to 1980 was renamed the Japan Housing Corporation—built dwellings that were rented or sold; and the Local Supply Corporation sold housing to the more needy classes. In most cases, plans were drawn up by the technical offices belonging to these agencies.[6]

In 1955, as a token of a renewed interest in Japanese culture, the Museum of Modern Art in New York inaugurated an exhibition entitled "The Architecture of Japan," with a catalog by Arthur Drexler.

In the same year, Tokyo's population reached 8 million. With the country still closed to immigration, the new workforce required by industry began to flow into the capital mainly from the poorest rural areas. The following year saw the promulgation of the Capital Region Development Law, an ambitious regional plan modeled on the 1944 Greater London Plan. Two satellite—or dormitory—towns, according to viewpoints—were proposed, according to the London model, as well as a greenbelt designed to limit expansion. The greenbelt was short-lived due to opposition from neighboring municipalities, which saw it as a hindrance to their own development.

In 1958, at a time when buildings did not exceed eight or ten stories, Tachū Naitō and Nikken Sekkei's Tokyo Tower appeared in Shiba-Kōen, one of the busiest areas of Minato-ku. This was a copy of the Eiffel Tower, slightly higher (333 meters) than its Paris counterpart, but with little of the engineering or pioneering allurement of the original. Planned as an antenna for telecommunications and brightly colored in accordance with the time's Aviation Law, the tower's two panoramic observatories are mostly frequented by tourists today; the tower constitutes a clear reference point in the center's chaotic skyline, forming a strong landmark, both night and day.

Another novelty—an experimental example of a single family house— also came in 1958: Kiyonori Kikutake's Sky House in Bunkyō-ku. On May 13th 1960, two years after it was built, Louis Kahn, who was in Tokyo for the World Design Conference, was invited to visit it. The Japanese architects attending the conference asked him a number of questions, and Fumihiko Maki stepped in as interpreter.

This was also the period in which, in association with Mori, Togo Murano won the competition for the construction of Yokohama City Hall, a large building in reinforced concrete. A similar concept was to be followed in the construction of The Waseda University Department of Literature (1962). It was a new time, a time in which tradition was rejected, and in

Kenzō Tange, *Plan of Tokyo for 15 million inhabitants*, 1961

which, with surprising naturalness, Japanese society and architectural culture seemed to thrive in modernity, through an unconditioned and uncritical assimilation of the American model. In short, what was happening in architecture was similar to what, in more general cultural terms, Takashi Furubayashi has called "stabilization of modern identity." But just one year later, the first signs of a shift from modernist orthodoxy came from Murano, with his Nihon Seimei Hibiya Building and the Nissei offices and theater (the latter was internally covered with an endless, scintillating mother-of-pearl mosaic). Many years later, the path he had chosen would result in a series of questionable buildings, including, for instance, the New Takanawa Prince Hotel in Shinagawa (1982).

The Sixties and Seventies

The capital continued its uncontrollable growth, becoming more and more chaotic: in 1960, Tokyo's population reached 9,676,000, with the entire metropolitan area, this figure rose to 12 million. Life within the city was getting hard, as well as expensive. For the first time, in the mid 1960s the population flow away from Tokyo was higher than migration into the city. Those who left the city did not actually abandon it: the suburbanization took place for entirely residential purposes, leading to a great increase in daily commuting. Moreover, the decentralization of residential settlements was still fostered by various administrations throughout the 1960s and 1970s, with intensive building of endless dormitory areas and fast metropolitan railroad lines. A series of new laws eased the sometimes complicated regulatory mechanisms of the residential property market: in 1962, divided ownership of property was authorized, making it possible to create normal condominiums; in 1963, height limits were radically increased, setting off the city's unstoppable process of high-rise development. Planners needed to make optimum use of the permitted volumes by unraveling a tangle of regulations, so they were often compelled to design irregular frameworks, following the equally irregular shape of the lots. The top floors thus featured odd, truncated pyramidal forms, in accordance with regulations concerning insolation. These buildings were to become an integral part of the disorderly contemporary urban scene.

It was in those years that Japanese architecture finally began to be included in Western architectural history, especially in writings devoted to the Mannerist trend or to feasible utopianism; years in which the *legenda aurea* of Japanese architecture took form. The leading European and American journals—from "Architectural Design" to "The Architectural Record," from "L'Architecture d'Aujourd'hui" to "Werk," from "Casabella-continuità" to "Baumeister"—dedicated a series of special numbers to the virtually unknown Eastern country and its exceptional rate of development: Walter Gropius, Udo Kultermann, Alison and Peter Smithson, Robin Boyd and others wrote about this new Japanese reality.

With his URTEC studio, Kenzō Tange, an influential member of the CIAM, was the uncontested leader on the scene. In 1960-61 he laid out his famous *Tokyo Plan for 15 million inhabitants*, a remarkable project for the development of the city over the bay. This utopian proposal, a re-formulation of a plan for the Boston bay, drafted just a year earlier for a community of 25,000 inhabitants, placed Tange at the hub of the architectural and urban debate around the city.

His plan retained the amenity of water, thus countering—both in concrete and poetic terms—a drastic project that had been presented three years earlier by the Japan Housing Corporation. Due to the scarce availability of land in the central areas, this former plan proposed dealing with the considerable increase in land value by using a system of dykes (much like in Holland) to reclaim land from the northern part of the bay

In May 1960, Tange fully described the philosophy of his proposal to architects from all over the world who had come to Tokyo for the World Design Conference.[7] Many reacted favorably to the proposal, but Zevi, who responded negatively, wrote: "Tange finally speaks of a fluid, open, democratic urban spatial order, but what he is presenting us with is so systematic and rigid that it cannot be realized in a free society. . . . he doesn't realize that his plan is simply adding a new chapter to the long sequence of 19th century utopian views of metropolises that thrive in the service sector."[8] But many years later, partially changing his mind, he was

Kenzō Tange, *Plan of Tokyo for 15 million inhabitants*, 1961
Detail of the directional axis, elevation and plan

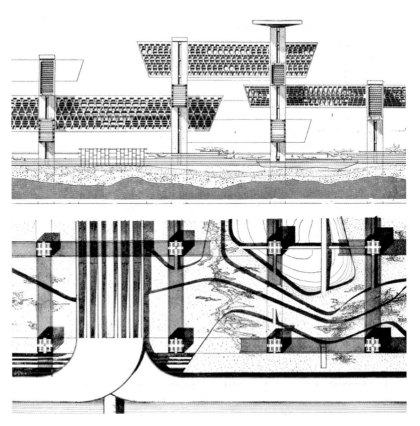

to write, with a habitual terseness that barely conceals his admiration: "From downtown studio flats to the directional axis that crosses Tokyo Bay, flanked by residential units. Mobility: three-level road system with links to the beltway and ramp connections. Enthralling spectacle of bridges suspended forty meters above the ground and fifty above the water. Interspersed towers that constitute a support frame for the building blocks, set 200 meters apart and rising 150-250 meters in height."[9]

The 1964 Olympic Games served as a great stimulus for urban planning; this was the first time they were to take place in Asia, and they had been eagerly awaited in Japan ever since the forced cancellation of the event in 1940. The Olympics showcased Tokyo to the world: hosting them was seen as an important opportunity for reaffirming the country's recovered national identity after almost two decades of severe psychological bewilderment brought about by the war. Japan's postwar rebirth charged the event with multiform political significance, which essentially came down to wanting to give the world a new image of the country and, above all, to free architectural culture from the restrictions of nationalistic ideologies and ties with tradition. Tange designed the National Gymnasium, or Yoyogi Sports Center (1961-64) for the occasion: a series of ambitious buildings devoted to sport, which remain surprisingly attractive and up-to-date even today. The general urban framework was cleverly devised: a circular basketball stadium and a large elliptical swim-

Kenzō Tange/URTEC, Yoyogi National Gymnasium, Shibuya-ku, 1964

ming stadium for 15,000 spectators (some of the pools can be converted into ice-skating rinks) set within Yoyogi Park, behind Omotesando station. The supple structures in reinforced concrete, conceived in collaboration with Yoshikatsu Tsuboi, are covered by bold roofs in catenary steel, suspended at the ends of huge ring-shaped reinforced concrete girders. The concavities opening up toward the exterior reduce the volumes, thus lowering air-conditioning costs and improving acoustics. It is a wonderful solution, similar to what Le Corbusier designed in 1958 for the celebrated Philips pavilion at the Brussels World Fair, and Eero Saarinen's plan for the New Haven Hockey Rink; but here, the work is on a much larger scale. The two main buildings of the complex also have a symbolic role: they act as a sort of legitimation for Japanese architectural culture to come onto the international scene, and they confirm its definitive break from the bonds of tradition.

Another building which is worth mentioning among the great number of other structures built for the Olympics is the Nippon Budōkan (literally "Japanese Hall for Martial Arts"): an octagonal building in reinforced concrete, covered by a metal structure and planned for 15,000 spectators. Although it was meant for judo, it also hosts rock concerts and other events; the Beatles played there in 1966. The architect Mamoru Yamada's idiom is relatively traditional; this was explicitly stipulated in the tender specification, due to the building's proximity to the Imperial Palace.

An intensive urban highway program was also drawn up in preparation for the Games. In an attempt to solve the worsening traffic problems, no corner of the city was spared, with the exception of the Imperial Palace. Kyōto and Ōsaka, which constitute the country's second largest metropolitan area, were provided with a high-speed railroad line served by the Shinkansen ("New Principal Line") trains, dubbed "bullet trains," which covered the 530-kilometer distance in three hours and ten minutes.

Despite the success of these costly undertakings, the city as a whole was beset by serious pollution. At that time, the Sumida was the most polluted river in Japan, children in Kawasaki City, one of the most highly industrialized suburban areas, were found to be suffering from respiratory problems.

Violent clashes between students and the police took place in 1968—exactly a century after the Meiji restoration, and Tokyo University remained closed for about a year. Tokyo, a city little inclined toward doubt and uncertainty, was forced to reflect upon the limits its very development entailed. At the same time, American involvement in the war in Vietnam, a relatively close country, created a rift in the faith it had just regained—with so much effort—in the United States.

The same year also saw the first Nobel Prize for Literature ever awarded to a Japanese, Yasunari Kawabata. The honor was welcomed as a form of recognition of the nation's regained cultural prestige. Two years later, at midday of November 25th 1970, Yukio Mishima, then 45 years old, carried out his prophetically awaited, dramatic ritual suicide ("seppuku" or hara-kiri) that he had described in detail in the short story *Patriotism*. Surrounded by the media, Mishima killed himself in the manner of a samurai, shouting "Tennō Heika banzai" ("ten thousand years of life to his majesty the Emperor") three times, to a hail of camera flashes and through a deafening noise coming from the helicopters of the television networks that had converged on the spot once the event had been announced. Less than a year and a half later, Kawabata, following his pupil's fate, was to commit suicide as well: both of them were possibly aware of the fact that "death is not the opposite of life but an integral part of it."[10]

At the beginning of the 1970s, the population reached 11.4 million. In order to reduce congestion in the central areas, the new towns of Tama, Kōhoku and Chiba—the satellite towns that had been announced over 20 years earlier—were finally built. Tama, in particular, is much more than a dormitory town. It contains the bizarre Sanrio Puroland, a large, covered entertainment park, financed exclusively by Japanese capital— a valid alternative to the Disneyland the Americans had built along Tokyo's western coast. It also features a number of unlikely residential quarters in German and Mediterranean styles. One of these, designed by Shōzō Uchii, is called "Belle Colline" and imitates a historical settlement perched on the Italian hills. "Tama is an example of this heterotopia resulting from utopian initiatives, a city of simulation, a city of placelessness."[11]

Arata Isozaki, Tsukuba Civic Center, Prefecture of Ibaraki, 1979-83

Finally, the science city of Tsukuba, in the distant prefecture of Ibaraki, was also built. This city, devoted to advanced science and technology and home to the great, new Tsukuba University complex, was planned in 1966. It took about 20 years to complete and contains 40 or so research institutes of national importance as well as large companies such as Canon and NEC.

During the 1950s, urban planning proposals included not only regional decentralization, but actual internal decentralization through the creation of alternative centers, first at Shibuya, Shinjuku and Ikebukuro, then at Ueno/Asakusa, Kinshichō/Kameido and Ōsaki, and finally on the artificial islands created in the bay. These plans were only carried out partially, but through the corollary of imposing infrastructure, they did actually lead to the transformation of the city into its current polycentric form.

The Heisei Boom

Tokyo reached unprecedented levels of prosperity due to its expansion in the 1980s, thus breaking all records. This was the Heisei Boom, the "bubble" that would not pop until the early 1990s. Economic growth drove the city well past its traditional sphere of influence; a high percentage of advanced services and financial interests were concentrated in Tokyo, which took it to the top of the league, firmly distancing it from the rest of Japan and placing it, as mentioned earlier, in a transnational system that included only a few global super-cities. Although the latter were in fierce competition, they were also complementary to one another and interacted strongly. Japan was the world's leading creditor and the greatest distributor of humanitarian aid to developing countries.[12] Fourteen of the fifteen largest banks in the world were based in Tokyo, and the whole Asian economic system, itself in rapid growth, linked in with it.

One at a time, a number of companies and buildings that symbolized American economy—from 7-Eleven to Firestone, from the Rockefeller Center to a good half of the Hollywood film studios—passed into Japanese hands, and the United States had to resign itself to this new state of affairs. When, in 1991, the 50th anniversary of the attack on Pearl Harbor was commemorated, the World War II veterans who had gathered at Honolulu for the event realized uncomfortably that they were practically forced to stay in Japanese-owned hotels.

In other words, although it did not have a role in the political or military spheres, Tokyo had become a massive economic and financial superpower that measured itself directly with London and New York, and often won the contest; unlike its two competitors, it also had an extensive, organized, efficient and productive workforce. Its stock market fluctuations had world repercussions, especially in the places, such as Los Angeles or São Paulo, where colossal Japanese investments were concentrated.

But the boom had its downside. The city was unwillingly forced to welcome increasing flows of often illegal immigrants, mainly from Taiwan and South Korea but also from Hong Kong and the rest of China, the Philippines, Thailand, Indonesia, India and even Iran.

Soon, concern began to arise over the giddy increase in prices and the consequent drain of large sectors of the population—especially the young—away from the downtown areas. The three municipalities of the CBD, the Central Business District,—Chiyoda, Chuo and Minato—tried to attract new residents by constructing luxury residential towers, but also by guaranteeing the presence of local amenities and retail outlets for the various neighborhoods. In short, the authorities were trying to counter the sort of phenomena that took place after the war in the downtown areas of American industrial cities, which were deserted in the evenings and on weekends. Yet, nothing of the sort really happened, at least not to American degrees; from this point of view, Tokyo remained closer to European cities.

With large percentages of middle- and low-income workers forced to daily commuting times of one or two hours, those years saw Minato-ku and the whole western hill belt of Yamanote in general become populat-

ed with high- and very high-income residents, including many wealthy foreigners. The CBD looked more and more like the sought-after downtown areas of Manhattan or London's West End, and Shinjuku became a new high-rise downtown. Moreover, some areas became specialized in offering the sort of services required by the upper classes, who were getting used to a more and more luxurious, compulsive and neurotic lifestyle. An example of this is the Roppongi area in Minato, as well as the fashionable neighborhoods of Aoyama and Akasaka. The high cost of residential property also led to cut down on the size of homes. Gregotti wrote: "Everything in Japan is very expensive, not just for foreigners, but even for most of the Japanese themselves, for whom the much-reviled Soviet standard of 12 sq metres of housing space per person would appear, in the world's most wealthy nation, to be an unreachable goal."[13] Indeed, the average surface area of an apartment was reduced from 57 square meters in 1980, to 49 in 1983 and 46 in 1987.[14]

Data related to property ownership is interesting as well, as it became prohibitive for wider and wider brackets of the population. In 1987, ownership levels in Tokyo stood at 54% compared with a national average of 64%.[15] But in the more expensive areas, these percentages were due to drop even more significantly. Rent accounted for at least 20% of salaries, compared with the national average of 15%.[16] A system of purchase on a 99-year lease contract was introduced. Between 1986 and 1987 the price of land for residential use rose by 95%, while land meant for business activities went up by 79%. Prices in the downtown areas were much higher than those of the major Western cities, even New York and London. The cost per square meter for an apartment in Chiyoda-ku, for instance, passed from an average of 33,480 dollars in 1986 to 46,256 dollars in 1987.[17] Such growth rates made it difficult for the metropolitan government to embark upon any kind of public works, be it houses or roads. The exceptional pressure constituted by the population, which was concentrated in a relatively small area of the country, also led to a number of further distortions, and any infrastructural action carried out to reduce congestion only seemed to give rise to other forms of congestion.

The lead role in the boom was played by the highly advanced building industry, which not only produced the buildings, but also the bold, costly

infrastructure: the artificial islands in Tokyo Bay, for instance, Kansai airport facing Ōsaka; the longest bridges on earth; and submarine tunnels, such as the 53-kilometer underwater passage linking Honshū with the northern island of Hokkaidō. In Tokyo there is the greatest number of bridges, viaducts and tunnels per unit of distance. An extraordinary productive machine. In the 1990s, with 3% of the world's population, covering 0.3% of the globe's surface, Japan produced 13% of the gross world product, second only to the United States. And a deeper analysis reveals that the building sector was responsible for an even more exceptional 17.9% of the gross domestic product, with a higher turnover than the European Union and the United States combined.[18] This is industry in the real sense of the term, and the stars featured in architectural journals had no say in this. In practice, it was—and is—monopolized by a small group of large multinationals (60% of the total) that employ thousands of different architects, engineers and technicians. These corporations have branches in the United States and Europe as well as throughout Japan, and operate all over the world. The formula is summed up by the phrase "design-and-build," which curiously links in with the Japanese term "kenchiku," meaning both "architecture" and "construction."[19] Design-and-build is reassuring for clients, as in practice they only have to deal with a single person who handles everything, including conception, planning, construction, finance and management. And if it is true that design quality has often suffered, we must acknowledge that these companies have made huge investments in research into advanced technologies, automation, sustainability, intelligent buildings, and so on.

Thus, projects became more and more ambitious and feasible, to the point that at the end of the 1980s a new proposal came up: the creation of an urban line between Tokyo, Nagoya and Ōsaka. The country's three major urban centers would be connected by the so-called "Maglev," high-speed trains (500 kilometers per hour) running on magnetic levitation, capable of covering the entire distance in an hour. This new, linear super-megalopolis was to be punctuated by highly-computerized "intelligent buildings" which were to house the country's vital economic and governmental ganglions, including the ministries: Delirious Tokyo.

Chinatown, Yokohama

Walkway, Makuhari Messe, Chiba-ken

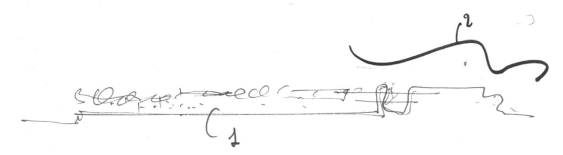

Renzo Piano, passenger
terminal, Kansai
International Airport,
1988-1994

The Crisis

Soon afterwards, the whole of Japan unexpectedly slid into a crisis. Serious episodes of political corruption emerged. In 1995, terrorism surfaced from a sinister and disquieting backdrop. The AUM Shinrikyō group—a faction described by Haruki Murakami in two of his books—attacked a subway train with nerve gas. Although there were only 12 casualties and a few thousand injured, the episode created huge shock that reverberated throughout the whole country.

Meanwhile, a real underclass was starting to populate Sanya, a neglected district in the municipalities of Taito and Arakawa; furthermore,

Shiodome,
Higashi-Shimbashi,
Minato-ku

many homeless took up their abode in Ueno Park and at Shinjuku station. Resignations and suicides (30,000 in 1998, 33,000 the following year) rocked the society to its core. The nation's competitivity, the highest in the world in the early 1990s, had dropped to between the 16th and the 18th place by 2000. This forced drastic cutbacks in urban and building projects of all types. It was mostly an economic crisis which only had a relative effect on the very high standard of living in Japan (still today, it is the richest country in the world).[20] Nevertheless, it has turned out to be very persistent and difficult to overcome.

Homeless in
Ueno Park

Shoeshiner, Shimbashi

Wooden dwelling, Sanya

[1] L. Benevolo, *Storia dell'architettura moderna*. Rome-Bari: Laterza, 1973, p. 831.

[2] Many years later, analyzing events, Yukio Mishima was to say: "Our Army's deep spiritualism has never been comprehensible to Americans". See T. Furubayashi, H. Kobayashi, *Le ultime parole di Mishima*. edited by E. Ciccarella. Milan: Feltrinelli, 2001, p. 81. Or. ed. *Saigo no kotoba*. Tokyo, 1970.

[3] F. Maraini, *Ore Giapponesi*. Milan: Corbaccio, 2000, p. 53. Orig. ed. 1956.

[4] A. Isozaki, "Città e architettura come rovina," in *Casabella*, no. 608-609, 1994.

[5] F. Maraini, p. 495.

[6] *See* I. Suzuki, S.M. Gold, "L'abitazione collettiva. Tipologie in evoluzione," in *Casabella*, no. 608-609, 1994.

[7] K. Tange, "Technology and Humanity," in *The Japan Architect*, October 1960.

[8] B. Zevi, "Costruiranno la capitale sulle palafitte – Piano regolatore per Tokyo," in *L'Espresso*, March 4th 1962. In support of the "new order" proposed by the plan, it is worth mentioning: G. Grassi, "La città come 'prestazione vitale', presentation to K. Tange, Un piano per Tokyo," in *Casabella-continuità*, no. 258, December 1961.

[9] B. Zevi, *Spazî dell'architettura moderna*. Turin: Einaudi, 1973, pls. 648-649.

[10] H. Murakami, *Tokyo Blues, Norwegian Wood*. Milan: Feltrinelli, 1995, p. 35. Orig. ed. *Noruwei No Mort*, Tokyo, 1987.

[11] H. Yatsuka, "Ecologia dei nuovi sobborghi di Tokyo. Tama New Town," in *Casabella*, no. 608-609, 1994.

[12] *See* T.R. Reid, "Japan," in *Architecture*, no. 10, 1996.

[13] V. Gregotti, "Una modernità dis-orientata," in *Casabella*, no. 608-609, 1994.

[14] *The Economist*, August 31st 1987. Cf. S. Sassen, *The Global City, New York, London, Tokyo*. Princeton: Princeton University Press, 1991, p. 275.

[15] Japan Economic Planning Agency, 1989. See S. Sassen.

[16] Tokyo Metropolitan Government, 1988. Cf. S. Sassen.

[17] See S. Sassen, p. 347. The value of the dollar in 1987.

[18] See F. Montagnana, "Il gigante in cantiere. Le 'big five' e le nuove frontiere tecnologiche," in *Casabella*, no. 608-609, 1994.

[19] F. Montagnana.

[20] See Data supplied by the International Monetary Fund on the "poverty index" i.e. the sum of the rates of unemployment and inflation, reported in *Il Corriere della Sera*, August 3rd 2003.

3. The Urban Structure

At first observation, Tokyo reveals two basic characteristics: firstly, it appears as a chaotic, cyclonic mass; secondly, it is formed almost entirely of new, or at least recently constructed buildings. What justifies the analogy with a cyclone is the city's chaotic, dynamic and boundless bulk, and the shock the unprepared visitor thus undergoes. In addition, everything seems to revolve, vortex-like, around an empty nucleus—the eye of the storm—formed by the Imperial Palace and the large park surrounding it. Enclosed by high walls and moats filled with water, it is a psychologically and physically inaccessible vacuum.

In a celebrated book by Roland Barthes, *L'Empire des Signes*, in a chapter entitled "City-center, Empty-center," he writes, "Quadrangular, reticular cities (Los Angeles, for example) produce what we might call a profound sense of uneasiness, they hurt our cenesthetic perception of the city, which demands that every urban space should have a center, a place we go to and come back from, a compact place to dream about, to which we are led and from which we can distance ourselves: in short, a place where we can invent ourselves. For a number of reasons (historical, economic, religious, military) the West has absorbed this rule all too well: all its cities are concentric. Moreover, conforming to Western philosophy, which regards each center as the seat of all truth, our town centers are always full. They are the places where the values of civilization are collected and condensed: values of spirituality (with churches), power (with offices), money (with banks), goods (with department stores) and words (with the 'agora': cafés and walks). Going downtown means encountering social 'truth', taking part in the sublime richness of 'reality'.

Hayashi and Yoshinaga, *Zoho edo oezu*, 1680

Ishikawa, Ryusen, Koosai and Gyokka, map dated 1748

The city I'm referring to [Tokyo] presents this amazing paradox: it does have a center, but this center is empty. The whole city revolves around a place that is both forbidden and indifferent, an abode masked by vegetation, protected by moats, inhabited by an emperor whom no one ever sees: literally, no one knows who does ever see him. Every day, with their rapid, forceful motion, taxis speed by like bullets, avoiding this ring, whose low rooftops—visible forms of the invisible—conceal its sacred nothingness. One of the two most powerful cities in the modern world is therefore built around an opaque ring of walls, water, roofs and trees. Its center is no more than an evaporated ideal whose existence is not meant to radiate any kind of power, but to offer its own empty center to all urban movement as a form of support, by forcing perpetual traffic detours. Thus, it appears as an image that unfurls again and again in endless circles, around an empty core."[1] To a Western mind, this disquieting vacuum might give rise to a sense of discomfort or, worse, to *horror vacui* ("fear of emptiness"), while instead it results more from the *horror plaeni* ("fear of fullness") that is part of a Japanese conception of aesthetics. Perhaps we can understand this conception better if we compare it to our appeasing concept of "silence" or, more precisely, to the Zen "silence of the mind," for which empty space is an excellent metaphor, as it paves the way for the spiritual conditions that are necessary for inner vision. Alternatively, it can be linked with a catalyzing, organizing function, analogous to the role played by the delicate fogs which often cover more or less extensive areas of the landscape in traditional Japanese paintings: an emptiness that "is not visible, but which is highly significant in formal terms."[2]

As for the second ingredient in Tokyo's character, the newness of its buildings, we must reiterate that it is hard to find any building over 100 years old. This might appear tragic to Europeans—especially Italians, who are used to associating architectural quality exclusively with buildings from the past—but could instead involve different, more subtle considerations, such as those propounded by Fumihiko Maki when, objectively, he observed: "The urban landscape is not weighed down by the past because here it is not allowed to build up. In this landscape of transition, human vestiges do not date back any further than a few decades."[3] In this sense too, the Japanese capital distinguishes itself from any other great historical capital in the world. It is not only different from European cities but also, for instance, from New York. Despite the fact that New York is often superficially associated with innovation, it was mainly between the end of the 1800s and the 1930s that its nucleus was actually formed. If anything, Tokyo is more similar to American cities such as Los Angeles or Houston, or recently expanded Asian cities such as Seoul, Shanghai, Hong Kong or Singapore. But it is much larger and more densely populated.

Therefore, contemporary Tokyo undoubtedly results from a casual attitude—to put it mildly—toward both demolition and building anew. We might say that the move to modernity—which, as mentioned earlier, coincides with the Meiji restoration—and everything that followed, was essentially marked by a huge, generalized process of demolition and reconstruction. Even so, despite the 1923 earthquake and its extensive destruction, the 1944-1945 war and the new building resulting both from post-war reconstruction and the huge expansion that took place throughout the second half of the 1900s (over 30% of Tokyo's buildings date back no further than 1985), the deepest essence of the city's urban structure has not been lost. As we shall see, it has simply been hidden beneath various new layers which appear exceedingly intrusive, thus preventing us from understanding the city at a superficial glance.

The historical framework

The ancient urban framework of Edo, a wooden city featuring a number of temples and sanctuaries, and housing the residences of the Daimyō, Hatamoto (the shōgun's standard-bearers) and Samurai, as well as the dwellings of workers and artisans, has survived remarkably well. Everything is concentrated more or less within the ring of the Yamanote metropolitan railroad line. As mentioned earlier, the feudal lords took up their quarters in Yamanote, or the High City perched on the hills west of the castle; the rest of the population was confined to Shitamachi or the Low City, the low alluvial, marshy lands, pervaded by rivers and canals, toward the bay to the east.

The castle occupied the summit of the Musashino plateau, where the Imperial Palace rises today. This is the heart of Yamanote, which is divided into three main parts: Jōhoku (north of the Kanda river), Jōsai (to the west) and Jōnan (to the south). But Yamanote is certainly not set on a flat, level plain; just like Rome, it is spread out on seven hills: Ueno, Hōngo, Koishikawa-Mejiro, Ushigome, Yotsuya-Kōjimachi, Akasaka-Azabu and Shiba-Shirogane, and at least five valleys are easily identified between the hills. This sloping land was ideal for the feudal aristocracy's residential settlements. The road network was strictly tied to the topography of the area: the main arteries ran radially along the crests of the hills, from the castle toward the outskirts, mostly heading east-west; the minor roads ran through the valleys. Still today, arterial roads such as Hōngo-dōri or Aoyama-dōri retrace the ancient paths and visibly follow the hill ridges, while on either side of these, other minor routes head down toward the valley floors.

In addition, several ring roads used to connect the radial roads. For instance, the road that today leads from the major Roppongi intersection

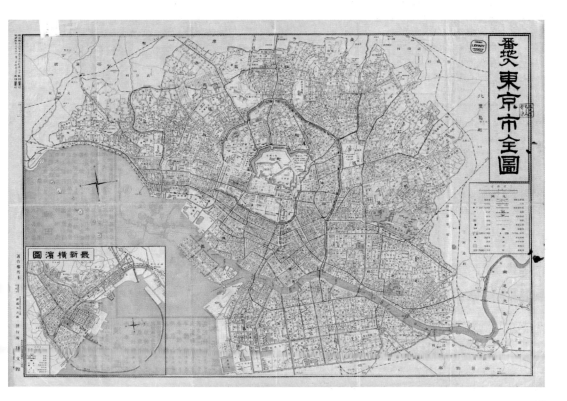

to Shiba Park, passing under the Tokyo Tower. Shiba Park lies exactly on the site of Zōjōji, one of the three temples erected to act as symbolic protectors of the city. The other two were Sensōji at Asakusa and Tōeisan Kan'eiji at Ueno. The respective positions of these three religious complexes followed Tao dictates. The Ueno temple in particular, built in 1625, corresponded to the "devil's gate," the access to the taboo quarters northeast of the castle.

On the whole, this structure is very different from that of European cities. It is supple and flexible, and follows the natural landscape; it has no walls or stone buildings; it is open and spreads out extensively over the territory; furthermore, it is easily adaptable to urban growth and the continuous modifications it brings about. But, above all, it is substantially a centrifugal structure, in contrast with the European centripetal tendency toward cities that are obsessively focused on their centers—places of maximum density, which hold all cultural and symbolic significance, and which, at least in the past, were closed in by walls and were clearly distinguished from the countryside surrounding them.

As Arata Isozaki observed, "No city in Japan is like European cities. In Europe, cities reflect the contrast with nature; nature and the city are two opposite concepts. In Japan, cities are like villages that have grown naturally from the 'power of nature'. In Europe, cities have a particular structure, what we call an 'urban' structure. In Japan we don't have such a structure."[4] As mentioned earlier, Barthes[5] himself has often pointed out that while the center of a European city is historically linked with a market or a cathedral where citizens converge, nothing so clear-cut ever occurs in a Japanese city. "Tokyo, thus, is an 'amoeba city' with its amorphous sprawl and the constant changes it undergoes, like the pulsating body of the organism. And as with an amoeba, Tokyo demonstrates a physical integrity and the capacity for regeneration when damaged."[6] This is a fascinating idea that is clearly linked with that of the "mollusc society" described by the anthropologist Chie Natane in reference to the "decentralized" psychological behavior of the Japanese as compared to the "vertebrate" behavior of Westerners.[7]

Often, settling in the Low City entails following strict regulations: the parcels the land is divided into—usually areas that are reclaimed from the waters—come from diversely oriented checkerboard systems measured in a square format of 60 ken (about 360 feet). This is the ancient system of territorial division known as "jōbō," also adopted, for example, in Kyōto where, unlike Tokyo, it is surprisingly easy to orient yourself. Moreover, the system is not exclusively used in the Low City. In Marunouchi, as well as the area comprising Sakurada, Shiba and Atago, where minor vassals had their hereditary habitations, today's framework has developed from a similar grid, but in a different way. The Banchō area is also measured and subdivided on the basis of similar modules: here, the grid is more evident than in the Low City, where over time, continuous urban growth has led to a significant increase in dimensions, practically erasing the grid. In Banchō it has also been proved that the grid ensured a view of Fuji from one of the hills, aptly named Fujimizaka (literally "the hill from which you can see Fuji"), now roughly the site of the Hōsei University campus.

But, generally speaking, the High City's uneven topography forced continuous exceptions, and the settlement system had to undergo continuous adjustments; irregularity was the norm. So residential settlements, which took up most of the area, developed from the relationship between a keen planning logic and the topographical diversity faced by the builders themselves. Unlike Europe, the city's architecture formed an intimate, fundamental relationship with nature. A notion of "topos" can be added to this, which results from the accumulation of an array of memories, religious meanings, and a complex and often mysterious stratification that took place at the time of the "genius loci." Thus, Edo was probably a beautiful city, situated on land of great scenic quality, a land of waters and uplands, endowed with luxuriant vegetation due to the high humidity and frequent rains, and dominated by the imposing, metaphysical presence of Fuji.

After the Meiji restoration in 1867, Japan's importation of Western modernity superficially destroyed almost all the sophisticated urban culture of the 17th and 18th centuries. Rivers, canals, ponds and sheets of water were often filled in or covered, the orography was changed, hills or valleys leveled, trees and woods cut down and even the names of places were changed. Indeed, accepting novelty entailed a very high price to pay. Something similar occurred in the artistic arena. The exposure to impressionism first and to the modernity of the historical European avant-gardes afterwards generated a serious crisis at the beginning of the 1900s, which saw the best Japanese artists divided between an often derivative imitation of Western styles and a retreat behind traditional methods. We ought to add that the sort of long "creative protectionism" which came about due to the fact that anything coming from abroad was shut out— a characteristic which belonged to the centuries prior to the Meiji restoration—doubtlessly contributed to delineating indigenous modes of artistic expression, which are as interesting as they are difficult to compare with what was happening in Europe at the time.

However, as we have said, the drastic revolutionary transformation of feudal Edo into modern Tokyo could not erase everything. Traces of its different past emerge everywhere in the contemporary city, even though recognizing these traces is getting more and more difficult year after year. From an architectural point of view, this means using European residential and monumental styles in the High City; meanwhile, a mechanical and sometimes naive superimposition of pseudo-European façades covers the commercial, artisanal and industrial styles of the Low City. Everything is marked by an uninhibited eclecticism that, even today, seems to be the cipher of Japanese planning culture. But the link that exists in Europe between architecture and cities is not to be found here; the continuous street fronts of the West will never be accepted in Japanese urban culture. In fact, a close look reveals that Tokyo has the same relationship between interior and exterior space as what is to be found in European urban planning.

On this basis, almost mechanically, the architectonic sign acts as a sig- nifier for the urban sign (using structuralist terminology from Louis Hjelmslev's connotative semiotics, as well as the transposition Renato De Fusco made of it)—on the condition, however, that we acknowledge the substantial difference that exists between the significance and the signi- fier of the historical Japanese and European architectonic signs.

Types of Settlement

Let's take a closer look at the three main categories of high-class residences that have existed throughout Edo's history—those of the Daimyō, the Hata- moto and, collectively, the warriors—and compare them with those of the lower classes in the Low City. The great houses of the Daimyō, the feudal lords who came from all over Japan but who were forced by the shōgun to take up their residence in Edo, easily provided the more modern city of the Meiji period with the expanses of land it needed for administrative, military and cultural buildings as well as dwellings for the new ruling classes. The Meiji restoration initially took possession of the large old res- idential estates and converted them into public buildings, embassies or new residences for the nobility and the high military hierarchies who moved from Kyōto to Tokyo with the new regime. Later on, in the first decades of the 1900s, many of these houses were subdivided further and transformed into greater numbers of smaller dwellings, or were torn down and rebuilt elsewhere to make room for new residential buildings.

At first there were vast green areas where houses and facilities for aris- tocratic families were laid out with archaic and Arcadian wisdom. Great attention was paid to their orientation and aspect—they invariably faced south, the direction where, according to tradition, the emperor's gaze was always directed—and to their location in relation to the water, springs, the greenery and the panorama. The main house was always in a raised position, while a small lake collected water in the lower part of the gar- den. Private roads ran through the large parcels, with a number of mi- nor buildings distributed along them. In a nutshell, these groups formed real neighborhoods, or small quarters, which were easily receptive to modifications and increases in density.

Consequently, Tokyo did not have to undergo the urban surgery that— sooner or later—became necessary in European capitals. Rather, it had to gradually adapt to the new needs that arose due to its continuous ab- sorption of Western influences, thus avoiding drastic operations such as those that took place in Haussmann's Paris, imperial Vienna and baroque, post-Unitarian or fascist Rome. This also underlies the absence of any form of classic urban design, any type of axial or prospective vision, any kind of authoritarian or "rational" system being imposed on the preexistent city. The urban structure of the High City has been modified continual- ly, without ever entailing the definitive loss of its old structure. Some of the contemporary city's best parks and gardens have descended from the ancient green areas of Daimyō residences, including the imperial gardens of Shinjuku, the Aoyama cemetery and the Shin-Edogawa park. And the historic framework of the Tokyo University campus, which today occupies

the ancient residence of the Maeda, lords of the Kaga province, can still be easily identified. The smaller houses of common folk and the (always numerous) temples mingled with the grand feudal residences. After the Great Meireki Fire, the temples were all moved to the city's central areas and placed along the main communication routes to form real suburban districts. In this case too, there is a clear difference from European cities, where religious buildings are invariably the gravitational center of the built-up area's overall structure.

Yamanote was somewhat similar to what we would call a garden city today. It was immersed in greenery, within a pastoral suburban landscape of alternating woodland and countryside, enhanced by evocative views toward the bay to the east and Fuji to the west. Hence, the feudal lords, even those who were so privileged as to be allowed to live inside the castle, built great, ambitious suburban residences. On the other hand, the lower classes, or tradespeople and craftsmen, built warehouses and opened workshops: this widely spread principle clearly explains the overtly class-conscious structure of the country's social tradition. The sort of class-mingling that came about in European cities was unknown in the Japanese urban structure, and so was the European aristocracy's type of urban settlement (for example, the Florentine or Roman Renaissance palaces from the 15th to the 17th centuries).

And although the feudal residences were poorly visible from the streets and enclosed by walls and gates, the trading settlements of the lower classes often tended to seem grander and more important than they were. This appears to have anticipated the contemporary image of the city's most popular areas, which today are made up of garish poster-buildings that—from an architectural viewpoint—transform façades into supports for advertisements, which are often larger than the buildings themselves: "The true form of urban architecture in Japan is a product of commoner culture."[8] It must also be said that the division of Edo into the High City and the Low City, and the prevalent attribution of the former to the aristocracy and the latter to artisans and merchants, is not only due to the fact that the High City is healthier and more beautiful. We must consider that with its rivers and many canals, the Low City featured an ideal water network for transporting goods.

The single-family living model—a house with one or maximum two floors, a well cared-for garden and a carp-filled pond—clearly derives from the feudal aristocracy's residential history, and is deeply rooted in all social classes, even if often it is only an aspire.

Land and property values are also tied to historic tradition. Still today, the High City features most of the desirable areas; within them, special prestige is attributed to properties occupying the historical sites of the great feudal residences. One example of this is the elegant hill of Mita Tsunasaka. On the southern side of the street, which runs east-west along the ridge, are the Mitsui Club and the Australian and Italian embassies, perfectly aligned, immersed in silence and greenery, and enclosed by beautifully cared-for boundary walls, following the scheme of the ancient aristocratic estates. The first two settlements share lands that were once under the jurisdiction of the Lords of Awaji. The Mitsui Club, a fine neo-Baroque villa designed for the Mitsui family's guests, was built by Josiah Conder in 1913 and has a double portico with seven barrel-vaults facing onto a Western-style garden. The Italian embassy occupies a particularly privileged compound, originally owned by the Matsudaira, Lords

Imperial Gardens,
Chiyoda-ku

of Oki, overlooking a classic Edo-period garden. Another adjacent Matsudaira residence is now occupied by the neo-Gothic campus of Keiō University. Not far away, at Mita Koyamachō, you experience the completely different atmosphere of an old, crowded, popular trading area. In the still vibrant neighborhood, you can find traditional shops and warehouses, including wooden structures; people living here used to transport their goods up and down the Furukawa river (today, the river is polluted and almost invisible under enormous, elevated highway strips).

In the aforementioned Banchō area there were a great many Hatamoto residences that were like smaller copies of the Daimyō estates. But here the gardens, which mostly faced southwards, were often modest; yet, they lacked none of the classic elements of the Edo period, and were gracefully conceived, with small artificial lakes and knolls. In this case too, at the time of the Meiji restoration the settlements came back into the hands of the central imperial power and were often used for the production of raw silk or tea, Japan's most highly exported products in those years. The lots that survived earthquakes, fires and wars have nevertheless been subdivided lengthwise, and there are few original buildings that are still identifiable.

Around 70% of Edo's residential fabric was occupied by warriors who ranked below the Hatamoto. Without going into the details of their complicated hierarchical divisions, it should be said that these areas have undergone minimal transformations compared with the former two categories. Many of the central residential areas will appear substantially unchanged to visitors, although a number of recent changes, such as plot divisions and certain typological choices, have been caused by high inheritance tax rates. At any rate, these houses became smaller and smaller, until they turned into tiny units within collective residences that looked somewhat like military barracks.

Examples of these kinds of communal residences were to found in Yotsuya and Ichigaya, west of the castle, and at Koishikawa, in the north, in the outskirts of Banchō. Many of these areas have recently undergone radical changes due to the construction of high condominium towers. This is one of the elements that rapidly led to a different orographic perception of the area, as it destroyed views of alternating hills and valleys, eliminating most of the green areas and closing off any panoramic vistas. In many cases, much of the High City's fascinating scenery has been lost, and any memory of it seems to have dissolved, as well. In others, in spite of the city's violent modernization, here and there certain high-quality elements have managed to survive. Take, for instance, the fashion districts of Aoyama and Azabu. These are exclusive, elegant residential areas, which Westerners find very enjoyable today. Yet, behind the night clubs, boutiques and showrooms, you can find quiet corners where the ancient framework is still recognizable, with its tiny valleys, small hills and well cared-for gardens. And although Azabu has unfortunately been damaged by a great number of overpasses, large parts of Aoyama still retain a totally Japanese grace and refinement, which is probably not very different from what is to be found in the trendiest, most experimental areas of West Los Angeles.

The main types of housing in the residential quarters of the Low City were defined and improved during the 1600s and 1700s. Two of them are clearly identifiable: the nagaya (literally "long houses") which date back to the 10th century, and the machiya ("urban houses") from the 14th century.

The former, which were meant for the lower classes, were, essentially, rows of efficiency apartments divided into two areas: one on the ground floor, which was used for working and cooking, and which featured a sunken fireplace (irori); and the other on a mezzanine story, covered with tatami mats and used both for eating and sleeping. These units fronted onto a double row, giving rise to a crowded, vibrant inner yard, marked by temporary constructions offering communal toilet facilities and often provided with small sanctuaries or votive altars.

The latter, an extension of the first type, were destined for the more well-to-do merchant class and were set on two floors around a private interior courtyard. The base module of 60 ken was reduced by 1/3, 1/2, or 2/3, according to the social status of the inhabitants. However, everything was very precarious, a characteristic that has always been present in the Japanese housing culture. On this point, Arata Isozaki reminds us: "in the Middle Ages, there was a concentration of activities going on in temporary constructions along the canals and river banks: just one flood, and everything was destroyed. There was no general order. These temporary structures were the harbingers of a sort of natural growth that greatly resembles chaos."[9] You can still feel the lively atmosphere of these areas. It's enough to move a short way from the great commercial arteries to find extremely fragile, small, even tiny houses which, from an an-

Aoyama Cemetery, Minato-ku

Yanaka Cemetery, Taito-ku

thropological viewpoint, are very interesting. In addition, you can find an archaic, minor semi-public or even private road network which brings to mind similar historical urban frameworks in the Mediterranean and Islamic worlds.

Mobility

You are immediately aware that driving in Tokyo, especially on its highways, is a dynamic, exciting experience that is extremely useful to get to know the city's contemporary values; traveling on the many overhead railroad lines is no different. The city's limitless size becomes apparent when, even on high-speed trains, the chaotic urban landscape accompanies the traveler for very long periods. When it comes to using the extensive subway metropolitan railroad network and its immense, super-crowded stations, it can become a powerful socio-anthropological experience.

It should be said however—somewhat paradoxically, considering the size of the conurbation—that experiencing Tokyo on foot gives a more concrete idea of the city's hidden urban structure. Walking along its streets and picking out its inner structure, hidden by the major road axes, the overhead railroad lines and highways, the bridges, viaducts and overpasses, by advertisements and brightly-lit signs, and by towers and other large buildings, may be a tiring, difficult experience, but it is certainly worthwhile.

It is thus clear that a dynamic fruition of the city constitutes a strongly distinguishing aspect of its urban structure. It can even be said that what is absolutely most striking to a visitor is Tokyo's infrastructure, which enables it to function reliably. Mobility is the number one concern, and solving problems connected with efficient road networks and transportation systems has always seemed to come—and still does come—before anything else. Referring to this, Gregotti has spoken of "a highly efficient transport system which must come to terms with conditions of mass mobility which border on a state of contradiction with respect to the availability of physical space."[10]

The railroad infrastructure is the most widespread and impressive feature of this transport system. Indeed, as Naomichi Kurata observes, "The history of urban development in Japan cannot be described without referring to the development of railway systems. Namely, it is said that most of the urban centers are not the product of the planning efforts of local or national governments, but rather the results of commercial activities or business strategies of railway related companies."[11]

In fact, Tokyo is at the center of a highly efficient, detailed network—the most sophisticated in the world, according to experts—of trains running above, below, and at ground level, of subway lines running long and average distances, all managed by JR, Japan Railways (a company born from the division and privatization of Japan National Railways) and a large number of private companies.

Furthermore, this network includes the high-speed trains, the aforementioned, famous Shinkansen, whose main stations (Tokyo, Ueno and

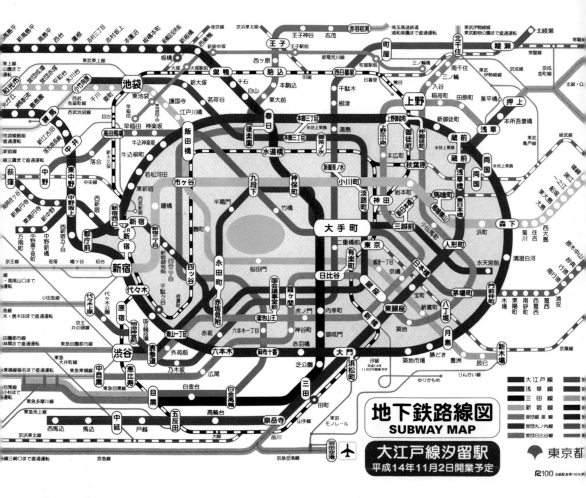

Subway map

Shinjuku) connect with the subway network. Every corner of the city—as well as the rest of the country—can be reached rapidly by train. Undoubtedly, the most important subway line is the Yamanote, a circular line run by JR which holds the world record in terms of daily passenger numbers and which creates a strongly perceived physical and psychological boundary between the part of the city it embraces—the capital's real center—and everything that remains outside. It forms the limit between the inner city and the suburbia, even though, in Tokyo, nothing can be so clear-cut. Apart from Tokyo Station, its circular route contains what are seen as the world's three most crowded stations: Ikebukuro, Shibuya and Shinjuku. The latter in particular, which has more than 60 exits, is also the station that handles the largest number of passengers in Japan, while Shibuya, where several of the city's major arteries converge in one multilevel intersection (the state road 246, the Shuto Expressway, the Meiji-dōri and the Roppongi-dōri), also hosts a terminus of at least 30 bus lines.

Seibu, Tobu, Odakyu, Keyo, Tokyu, Keisei and Sotetsu, just to mention the principal private companies operating in the city's metropolitan area, are often part of financial groups whose activities include department stores, supermarkets, hotels, land development, building firms, travel agencies, advertising agencies and holiday management.[12]

For instance, Tama, the garden city southwest of Tokyo, was mainly developed by the Tokyu Corporation, one of Tokyo's largest companies, founded in 1918. This garden city was originally planned to hold 400,000 inhabitants, as well as the central nucleus of Shibuya. The competition triggered between the various private companies has often led to gigan-

National Road no.1, Minato-ku

Following pages: Shimashi, Minato-ku

tic development. Take, for example, the case of the historic rivalry between Tokyu and Seibu, which has generated a chain of investment in the retail sector. Seibu, which is innovative and led by "ideas," owns the Seibu department stores as well as the PARCO centers: elegant buildings devoted to fashion, full of boutiques, restaurants, coffee bars, art galleries and cinemas. The more conservative Tokyu (led by the "market") has responded to PARCO with Fashion Community One-O-Nine, and to the department stores with its own, extremely well-known Tokyu Hands.

Thus, significantly, the stations and their immediate surroundings tend to transmute into extensive multifunctional structures which take up considerable portions of the city with their multiple exits, their large areas for services, shopping and catering, and their colossal walls filled with advertisements. They are "animated underground labyrinths overfilled with goods" in which "you feel the city is governed by the laws of economics, where chaos and a complete lack of interest in physical quality or the planning of space go hand in hand with functionality, efficiency, vitality and comfort."[13] If you do not look at the signs, it is hard to find your bearings. Due to such disorientating interchange junctions between cars and trains, or between different trains, you often have no idea which level you are on and whether you are above ground or below. If you do not know which exit to take, you risk finding yourself a long way from where you want to be. Even once you are outside, it is not always easy to identify what the basic street level is. Multiple levels are the norm; cars speed by above you and/or way below you, and you feel you are living in a futuristic sketch. In general, the notion of "ground floor" or "street level" often becomes chaotic. More and more frequently, the "ground floor" tends to be a multi-floor "packet" that links orographically different levels, but what's even more important, it is sinking deeper, on a quest for space, which is increasingly vital.

Predictably, Tokyo also records the heaviest air traffic in Japan. (The second place goes to the Osaka airport system, which includes Kansai, which was designed by Renzo Piano on an artificial island in the bay.) The city's principal airports are Narita, which is mainly for international flights and lies in the Chiba prefecture, its two terminals decorated with great murals by Ikkō Tanaka; and Haneda, on an island facing the bay at the mouth of the Tama river, the Tokyo-Yokohama center of gravity, mainly used for domestic flights. Haneda is much nearer the downtown area, to which it is also connected by a monorail. Passenger traffic across the city's two airports taken together is astounding; it is the heaviest in the world, followed by London, Atlanta and Chicago. The traffic density at the Haneda terminal alone holds the third place worldwide, after Atlanta and Chicago.[14]

If the line linking the capital with Narita has led to gigantic development along the coastal strip that extends east and then south into the prefecture of Chiba—which includes the cities of Urayasu, Ichikawa and Narashino—then Haneda's presence has generated the development of over a thousand companies, forming a huge industrial estate. In their turn, these companies lie at the root of the hardware center that has transformed the central part of southern Tokyo and, on the other side of the Tama river, of a High-tech research and development center in Kawasaki, where plants belonging to a large number of high-tech companies such as Hitachi and Fujitsu are based.

There are essentially two harbors, in fierce competition with each other: the port of Yokohama and the Tokyo Harbor itself. The former (which, historically, has always functioned as Tokyo's port) is a large, natural basin enclosed by the two branches of the Shuto Expressway. The Tokyo Harbor, which was only opened in 1941, is crossed by the above-mentioned Expressway, as well as by the spectacular Rainbow Bridge. Nevertheless, its shallow waters do not allow access to the largest ships. Bridges, skyscrapers and a copy of the Statue of Liberty set on a small island highlight its resemblance to the New York Bay. Unfortunately the canal, which used to be the Low City's trading route, retains no more of its historic mobility.

On the other hand, the road networks deserve careful consideration. One of the characteristics of the old, lost feudal framework is a system that was originally conceived to slow down the enemies' approach

to the castle, by putting the largest possible number of physical obstacles in their way. Thus, there are endless street corners created by closed lots set between one road axis and another. Even today, despite its modernity, the city's secondary road network is full of breaks and interruptions, sharp turns and continuous changes of direction. It is no different from what happens, on a much smaller scale, among the "calli" in Venice: it is a sort of "snakes and ladders," the "sugoroku" which Hidenobu Jinnai refers to.[15] In short, there seems to be a total lack of the all-encompassing design that defines many European capitals. "This contrast is evident in the comparison of Paris and Tokyo. Paris is a city divided with foresight into parts 'cut' from the whole, while Tokyo follows the sense of the whole enveloping all its various parts. Paris is a splendid, beautiful city, indeed, but may be encountering difficulty to adjusting to the needs of the 21st century. Its masonry architecture makes it, in a way, a static and inorganic monument of the past. Tokyo, however, remains a synchronic whole, tenaciously surviving by rather amoebic adaptability. It is an ugly, chaotic metropolis, but it is organic and constantly in the throes of change. I cannot help wishing at times that the amoeba would replicate its parts with somewhat more care, but its vigor cannot be denied."[16]

The current road network is, therefore, impenetrable, confusing and, as we have seen, it practically lacks any large axes. (Something resembling a square-shaped grid only appears in the Ginza district, around Tokyo Station, and in a few other areas.) "Even though" as mentioned earlier, "Japan has imported grid models from China (in the cities of Kyōto and Nara, for example), buildings do not face onto the street; they are surrounded by greenery, like in a village; they are not connected with each other and they do not create an urban space."[17]

The cardinal points used for American cities and place names—maybe as part of the country's pioneering heritage—are of no use. Ad-

dresses do not follow this system, which is widespread almost everywhere else in the world. The street is not perceived as a complete entity in itself, with a beginning and an end, so it doesn't have a name. Some of the great avenues ("dōri") are only a recent exception; they have been named only to follow Western usage, and in any event, they are not used in addresses. Instead, aside from the name of the township, indicated by the suffix "ku" or "shi", addresses only have three numbers: the "chome," a sort of neighborhood or small quarter subdivided into different blocks; the block and the building itself, which is often numbered chronologically according to the date it was built, and not gradually, by physical position.

This unusual system did not escape Barthes, who wrote, "The roads of this city do not have names. Of course, there is a written address, but it only has a postal value. It refers to a land register (through totally non-geometric quarters and blocks) and will make sense to the postman but not to the visitor. The largest city on earth is practically unclassified, the spaces that make up its details are unnamed. This residential annulment seems quite inconvenient to us, as we are used to thinking that what is most practical is also most rational (according to this principle, a street number is the best way to name a place, like in the United States or Kyōto, a Chinese city). Tokyo, instead, tells us once more that rationality is just one of several systems. . . . This city cannot be known except through some sort of ethnographic activity: you need to find your bearings , , , by walking its streets, by looking around you, through habit and experience: each discovery is both intense and fragile, it cannot be repeated, and only its trace can be left in our memory: in this sense, visiting a place for the first time is like starting to write about it: as the address has not been written down, it has to found its own writing."[18]

Squares like Italian piazzas do not exist. This is not to say that there are no great, wide spaces or openings at road intersections or at accesses to bridges, but that these areas never feature a recognizable design. The role played by the Italian piazza, a social point of reference, was once present around the walls of Tokyo's sanctuaries; now, the stations have probably taken their place.

These are the true cruxes of the urban dynamics, around which the quarters and parts of the city are orientated and given hierarchical order. Again, it is Barthes who points out that, "in this immense, truly urban territory, the name of every quarter is clear and well-known, it is marked on the rather bare maps (since there are no street names) like a great flash; it assumes the highly significant identity that, in his own way, Proust explored in 'Place-Names'. If the quarter is so clearly delimited, concentrated, contained, closed in its own name, it is because it has a center, but this center is spiritually empty: usually, it is a station."[19]

The result is that Tokyo is now a labyrinthine, magma-like whole, apparently built without order, hierarchy or form. A double, suspended network of railroads and highways, created to reduce traffic at intersections, is superimposed on a sort of intricate grid made of small, continual, almost topologically deformed rotations, as if the grid itself had been designed on a sheet of rubber which was then stretched and pulled in various directions.

The city's largest, most imposing structure, however, is actually one of the largest and most impressive urban structures in the world: the Tokyo Metropolitan Expressway. This gigantic strip of highway in reinforced concrete and steel, which often intersects the railroad viaducts, envelops the capital for over 220 kilometers, sometimes running way overhead, some-

Yurakucho Station

Monorail

Shinkansen

times underground, connecting it to the suburbs and the more distant cities of Yokohama, Saitama and Chiba. The Expressway crosses residential and industrial quarters, old streets and new, rivers and canals; it takes no notice of parks, landscapes, buildings. . . . The piers on which it rests, which are up to 40 meters high, have been made even more intrusive by aseismatic regulations (usually roadways are allowed a 20-centimeter oscillation). Although the Expressway causes high noise and visual pollution, we must also add that, unlike elsewhere, the spaces underneath it are surprisingly clean and usually have regular usage patterns. The first tract, between Chuo-ku and Minato-ku, was completed in 1962—early, compared with the goal of connecting the various sport facilities built for the 1964 Olympic Games.

At any rate, Tokyo's many old canals, often marked out by green areas, small panoramic spots and idyllic rest areas, have paid the highest price: forming natural riverbeds, free of buildings and encumbrances, most of them were invaded by the Expressway. The highway did not even spare Nihonbashi, the most famous of the historical bridges in the heart of the city which, in its current form, dates from 1911. Decorated with bronze lamps protected by mythological lions (karakishi) and deer (kirin), it now seems to disappear into the gigantic contemporary structure's shadow.

In short, we can therefore say that the overall structure of the contemporary city is probably the result of a multifaceted and unique process of hybridization between the ancient structure of old Edo and the careless importation of modern Western teachings. Such a process has produced ambiguous "innovation" that is hard to identify, disquieting and disagreeable in many ways, but that is undoubtedly also fascinating, fluid and easily adaptable. "And the reason why Tokyo is so extensive is that it has never had a plan, a center or visible order. The result is that Tokyo is 'used' today just as it was in the past."[20]

[1] R. Barthes, *L'Empire des Signes*. Geneva: Skira, 1970.

[2] G.C. Calza, *Stile Giapponese*. Turin: Einaudi, 2002, p.22.

[3] F. Maki in *Saper credere in architettura, trentadue domande a Fumihiko Maki*, edited by L. Spita. Naples: Clean, 2003, pp. 23-24.

[4] A.Isozaki, in *Saper credere in architettura, trentadue domande a Arata Isozaki*, edited by L. Spita. Naples: Clean, 2003, p. 9.

[5] Cf. R. Barthes, op. cit.

[6] Y. Ashihara, *The Hidden Order, Tokyo through the Twentieth Century*. Tokyo-New York: Kodansha International, 1989, p. 58 Or. Ed. *Kakureta chitsujo*. Tokyo: Chūōkōron-sha, 1986.

[7] Cf. C. Nakane, Tate *shakai no rikigaku* (*Dinamic of the vertical society*). Tokyo: 1978.

[8] H. Jinnai, *Tokyo, A Spatial Anthropology*. Berkeley-Los Angeles-London: University of California Press, 1995, p. 28. Or. Ed. Tokyo: 1985.

[9] A. Isozaki, op. cit., p.15.

[10] V. Gregotti, "Una modernità dis-orientata," in *Casabella*, no. 608-609, 1994

[11] N. Kurata, "Lo spazio in concorrenza. Ferrovie private e sviluppo urbano," in *Casabella*, no. 608- 609, 1994.

[12] Cf. N. Kurata, op.cit.

[13] C. Baglione, "*Quattro passi nel contesto*," in *Casabella*, no. 608-609, 1994.

[14] ACI (Airports Council International) data, September 2003.

[15] Cf. H. Jinnai in "Process: architecture," no. 72, 1987 = *Ethnic Tokyo*. Tokyo: 1987.

[16] Y. Ashihara, op.cit., p. 43.

[17] A. Isozaki, op.cit., p.14.

[18] R. Barthes, op.cit., 43-46.

[19] Ivi, p. 47.

[20] A.Izozaki, op.cit., p. 14.

江戸名所一覧雙六

Hiroshige, Edo Meisho
Ichiran Sugoroku, picture
of Edo

Following pages: Sugoroku,
Snakes and Ladders, Mejii
period

4. The Japanese Situation

Tradition and Innovation

Daniel Libeskind once said, "I think that the cultural problem of Italy is isolation. When I go to Italy, I always think that Italy and Japan are very similar countries, in the sense that they are islands of a certain sensibility; they seem to try to immunize themselves from the developing transitions, the changes that are happening under their own noses."[1] Libeskind knew Italy well, having lived for several years in Milan, but he also knew Japan, where he had just built a remarkable structure— and he is probably right.

His words introduce us to the first, contradictory aspect of the Japanese situation, that of its difficult relationship to the new. If it is true, as has been noted many times, that Japan is the most forward-looking country in the world—perhaps in many ways more so than the United States and the countries of Northern Europe—it is also curiously true that it puts up an extreme resistance to the new. Its history, particularly as regards architecture, can be read as an on-going resistance to anything new arriving from abroad, threatening the survival of its indigenous culture and traditions.

Ancient roots lie at the base of this attitude. For a long time China was the country that most influenced Japan. The introduction of Buddhism—which resulted from contact with Korea in the middle of the 6th century—and especially other esoteric sects, led to the construction of Chinese-style temples, which subsequently led to substantial changes in non-religious architecture. In Tokyo, the most ancient of these structures is believed to be the ruins discovered in Kokubunji City, a building erected by order of the emperor Shōmu in 741. The adoption of the new from China provoked the first loss of traditional historic values, often psychologically perceived as a more general and real loss of identity. Japan tried to resist, as the ancient slogan *wakon kansai* ("Japanese spirit, Chinese awareness") demonstrates.

With the Meiji restoration (the "restoration" of this imperial dynasty would, in cultural terms, have been more aptly called a "revolution") and the opening up to the West—and the new—that followed, Japan was soon exposed to the risk of being overrun a second time, this time by European culture. Once again the desire for renewal conflicted with the fear of irreversible loss of identity. The slogan became *wakon yosai* ("Japanese spirit, Western awareness"). In other Asian countries exposed to the same dilemma, the phrase was (in China) "Chinese identity, Western functionality" or (in Korea) "Eastern values, Western functionality."[2] Indeed, the fears of these Eastern societies were not unjustified. Within just a few decades the majority of them were to end up under the yoke of Western (or, perhaps more precisely, American) cultural imperialism. In architecture, reactions were not slow in coming and were often regionalist in tone, in an attempt to combine modernity with local traditions. They were not that different from those in countries on the periphery of the West, such as Finland's national Romanticism, or Catalan Modernism, which, as is well known, has little of the modernist about it.

The strong contrast between the old and the new was clearly recognized by Bruno Taut, writing in 1935: "Japan is currently undergoing a particularly intense conflict. Tradition, which has always informed everything in minute detail, remains alive and well and retains a strong following among the large majority of the population. At the same time, the life of the country is coming under the influence of Western technology and civilization, and the forms and modes of Western life. This evolution, which is possibly not entirely desired, has real relevance. It matters little if, thus far, only a slim proportion of architectural structures are modern, for it will be these few examples of the new trend that will determine architectonic development for decades to come."[3] This was a prophetic conclusion, destined in substance to occur quite rapidly, despite much resistance. But that does not mean that the arrival of modernity was easy and painless. Consider, for example, what Kenzō Tange, a person certainly not suspected of reluctance towards the new, was to say approximately twenty years later: "Immediately after World War II, up until the 1950s, Japan struggled to reconstruct its economic and physical infrastructures. The thoughts of the Japanese were directed backwards, fixed on ancient traditions and their history. In this atmosphere architects felt that they would not satisfy the spiritual needs of the populace if their architecture was not inspired by ancient Japanese traditions."[4]

In Japan this resistance coincided with a more general opposition to everything coming from other countries, the West in particular. Their relationship with Western culture was therefore always difficult and con-

Wooden buckets

Fountain of a temple

Refreshment point

104

Stamp for ideograms, Gallery of Hōryōji Treasures, Taito-ku

troversial. On the one hand there was clearly a certain inferiority complex in relationship to Europe—architecture included—but on the other this complex was tempered by their recent but growing level of self-awareness. Here the Japanese had much in common with the Americans. But in Japan, unlike in America, this self-awareness was tinged by a cultural chauvinism whose roots dug deep into an ancient culture.

On a social level, even if Westerners, and Europeans in particular, are regarded very highly, it is also true that they remain *gayjin* (foreigners)—and this term always has a slightly pejorative tone. Also, even though the Japanese are extraordinarily kind towards guests, one should nevertheless not forget the speech made by the philosopher Jacques Derrida at the "Any"—"Anywhere" conference held in 1992 on Yu Fuin Island, located in the southern part of the country.

The famous French philosopher's text, entitled *Faxitexture*, analyzed the two correlated concepts of *hospes* and *hostis* (guest and enemy). It also cited Kojève, the author who saw the end of history taking shape in modern Japan, at least in the Western sense of the concept, which had occupied European thinking at length during the eighties. It then discussed the notion of "anywhere," the theme of the conference, and its dual interpretation as "from nowhere" and "from somewhere."[5]

Signs and Language

It is probably true that any attempt to penetrate a culture characterized by elusiveness is a hard battle, if not one lost at the outset. A book entitled *16 Ways to Avoid Saying No* by Massaki Imai became famous when it attracted the attention of Derrida in a Tokyo tourist bookshop. Indeed, any Westerner who has experienced speaking with the Japanese will have become aware of the difficulties encountered by his interlocutor when having to contradict or simply admit to not being in agreement, and the hesitant strings of words that etiquette demands in such an embarrassing situation. The Westerner encounters identical problems in understanding that, beyond these strings of words and kind phrases, the answer is, in fact, "no." Another example comes from the strong, om-

Magazines

nipresent use of "I" in Western languages. In Japanese this becomes a subtle, variable concept, which, when it cannot be entirely avoided, may be designated in twenty-six ways depending on the different "positions" of the subject.

Linguistic differences certainly form an important aspect of the question. "The structure of the Japanese language—in which the meaning of a word depends, to a great extent, upon the 'context' in which it is used—perhaps offers a key with which to explain the type of cognitive attitude required by the Japanese reality. Japanese is, in fact, a language with a weak grammatical and syntactic structure, characterized by ambiguities, multiple meanings, a wealth of images in which, with respect to Western languages, more space is left for the intuition of the listener, and autonomous 'islands' of meaning are grouped around weak logical nodes."[6] Hence it is a language without the logocentric base of Western thinking and thus one that shows itself to be exactly what it is: a branch of Chinese thinking.

Japanese writing demonstrates equally important differences. Its complete indecipherability, its aesthetic leanings and its invasive presence are notably apparent. First of all there is a very strong graphic "presence": each sign is like a microcosm of fascinating, autonomous meaning. But there is also a simpler physical presence that is almost as strong: signs are practically everywhere. Roland Barthes observed that "le mur est détruit sous l'inscription" and entitled his already much cited book

Road signs, Roppongi

Luminous signs, Shinjuku-ku

on Japanese culture *L'Empire des Signes*. "The Empire of Signs? Yes, if you mean that these signs are empty and that the ritual is godless."[7]

Much of what is written—at least in Tokyo and the other major cities—in fact reassuringly appears in English translation. But it may be just this that underlines and accentuates the dissimilarity: Japanese script is too different to avoid the rising doubt that behind it lies a profound difference in thought. In contrast to the practical, concise and restricted Latin alphabet, Japanese script comprises two different systems, which somewhat confusedly interact with each other. Most importantly, however, while the first one, not unlike those from other "phonetic" civilizations, such as India or Islam, translates sounds into signs, the second adds a specifically representative aspect.

As is generally known, the forms of writing are *kanji*, of Chinese origin, which uses polysemic ideograms, and *furigana*. The former is a system essentially based on diversity: hidden within the very large number of ideograms, which take on different meanings in different syntactical contexts, there nest, almost like invisible ghosts, infinite different and often obscure concepts.

The latter, *furigana*, is subdivided into *hiragana* and *katagana*. Hiragana is a phonetic, syllabic transcription of *kanji*, which comes into play to simplify the reading of difficult or little used words; *katagana* is the phonetic transcription of the many words borrowed from Western languages, primarily English. When these words are written using

the Latin alphabet, the term used is *romàji*, which contains the root of the word "Rome."

Even the most cultured of Japanese knows that around 40,000 signs are not mnemonically controllable: this is an integral part of a more or less articulate awareness of the epistemological "irreducibility" of the world. Tokyo, as Geert Bekaert observes, reiterating Barthes' writings, "reminds the Westerner that the rational is merely one system among others."[8] The city and its language constitute the most effective symbolic metaphor of the labyrinthine, flexible, Babel-like unfathomability of what is real.

Refreshment point windows

Religious Thought and Daily Ritual

Underlying the Japanese spiritual identity are three significantly inter-related phenomena: the national Shintō religion, Zen philosophy and the tea ceremony. The first, an animist cult in which *kami* (natural divinities) inhabit objects and phenomena, entails diverse forms of pantheism as well as the belief that the emperor is of direct divine descent. Such linking of God and monarch occurs frequently in the history of humanity and many civilizations in the past were founded on such an assumption. Shintoism also often easily cohabits with Buddhism and other forms of worship.

In architectural terms, animism translates into great attention towards the cyclical aspect of nature, but also its indirect lesson on the layout of buildings within a meaningful whole and the routes linking them.

Zen, whose name derives from the Chinese *ch'an*, which is in turn a phonetic transcription of the Sanskrit *dhyana* (meditation), was introduced from the Asiatic continent in the 12th century through two sects, Rinzai and Sōtō. Without going into speculation or deep cognitive argument, it makes use of meditation and other esoteric practices to reach

Monks at the entrance to a temple

Mariko Mori, *Tea Ceremony III*, 1995

nirvana, and sudden, explosive inner enlightenment. Unorthodox and ineffable by its very nature, it is difficult to say whether Zen is of Buddhist leaning or not. It is perhaps most usefully compared with a school, a faith, a way (*Tao* in Chinese, *michi*, *dō* in Japanese). The interest in self-discipline and actions rather than words brought about its widespread diffusion, especially among the warrior classes.

"Zen, in its completeness, engages in battles against every abuse of power of the senses. It is known that Buddhism eludes the inevitable route of every assertion (or negation), recommending never to be prey to the four following propositions: *this is A*; *this is not A*; *this is at one time A and not-A*; *this is neither A nor not-A*. This quadruplicate possibility corresponds to the perfect paradigm as created by structural linguistics (*A, not-A, neither A nor not-A* [zero grade], *A and not-A* [complex grade]). In other words, the Buddhist route is exactly that of the obstructed senses: the same mystery of meaning, the paradigm, is rendered *impossible*."[9] "All Zen thinking . . . seems like an immense practice dedicated to the *suspension of language*, the breaking of the sort of internal radiophonics that continually resonate within us, even when sleeping (perhaps this is why apprentices are kept from falling asleep). It is a practice dedicated to emptying, to disconcerting, to drying up the unstoppable chattering of the soul. Perhaps what Zen calls *satori*, a word for which Westerners have no translation apart from vaguely Christian terms such as illumination, revelation or intuition, is none other than a panicked suspension of language, the white-out that annuls the reign of Codes within us, the breakdown of that interior recital that constitutes our persona. Now, if this state of *non-language* is a liberation, it may be so because in the Buddhist experience the proliferation of thought to the second power (thinking about thinking) or, if you prefer, the infinite addition of innumerable meanings (a circle in which language itself is the depositary and model)—all this is regarded as an im-

Zen Garden

pediment. Instead it is the abolition of thinking about thinking that breaks the vicious infinity of language."[10]

Zen has also deeply permeated the Japanese aesthetic, and its influence can be found in every artistic sphere. Art is never embellishment or decoration but the terrifying depth of the spirit of man, illumination, salvation. Zen also involves strong interest in "nothingness," the concept of emptiness and the spatial dialectic between full and empty. In addition, Zen temples—a distinct architectural style first appearing in 1202, creating extensive complexes, often true monasteries—still form an exemplary illustration of the relationships between architecture and the natural context, between building and garden, between artifice and nature.

Student

Two important examples are the Jizō Hall (1407), situated to the north of Tokyo where it borders the prefecture of Saitama, and the Relic Hall (first half of 15th century) in Kamakura. Moreover, the compositional methodology of a Zen garden has undeniable resonance with much recent contemporary architectural aesthetic. This is seen in its progressive levels of abstraction, its sophisticated use of space and, especially, in its main function of rendering contemplation of the "internal" nature of man's mind possible, carrying out the same role as the fog or blank spaces in pictures.

Even though it is an intense aesthetic experience, the tea ceremony, which in Japanese is more simply called cha-no-yū (hot water for tea), should nonetheless not be regarded simply "as a pastime with aesthetic leanings, but as a vehicle created by man to keep himself alert, so that he does not become drowsy by automatic repetition of practical activities and so lose contact with the intrinsic value of his deeds and his own spiritual reality."[11] The aim is internal growth: "For this reason, as is emphasized in Zen philosophy, Japan has created arts that neither have practical purpose, nor offer aesthetic pleasure, but represent an apprenticeship of consciousness and must serve to bring it towards the fi-

School students

Ex voto, Zojoji temple

nal reality."[12] This, in rarefied and often elliptical manner, is what Kaku-zō Okakura described in his celebrated *The Book of Tea* (1906).

Beyond the doubtless fascination that all this can instill in Western sensibilities, we must ask ourselves whether, and to what extent, architectural planning can profit by it. Bruno Taut, a leading player in a still strong, self-confident modernity, observed: "I do not want to contest the great influence that local traditions have on architecture, but such things can only be understood by the Japanese, therefore they remain sterile for the renovation in architecture that is taking place all over the world. But I believe that they are sterile for the latest developments in Japanese architecture as well. Let us consider—and this may seem a sacrilege to many Japanese—the teahouses with their salons for the tea ceremony. Their great beauty is beyond debate; nevertheless this in itself is useless to a modern Japan. It is no longer architecture, but poetic improvisation so to speak. Yet this lyricism is not easily transmitted to the wood, the bamboo, the *shoji*, the mats, the stucco and so forth. The old masters of the tea ceremony stressed the pure, intimate beauty of this atmosphere. They declared that it would be lost in repetition, and they would certainly find every aspect of one of today's teahouses to be second-rate: the atria formed by trees left in their natural state, the stucco applied to the bamboo, the rustic fencing, the irregular stones in the garden—and the garden itself with its thousands of imitations in hotels, restaurants and private houses. . . . What should have been a singular expression of contemplative nature, of spirituality and personality, has been transformed into a series of rules set in stone and arid academicism. And this refers not just to the architectonic elements but the ceremony itself."[13]

If therefore, together with the Shintō religion and Zen thought, the tea ceremony constitutes the third, and most difficult lesson for architecture, this should be limited—and this is no small thing—to the careful examination of man's movements in space, to his continuity over time,

to the function of light and to the infinite possible variations within a space (that of the hut or the tea room), which from many points of view is aesthetically minimalist. And, even in this case, the relationships between the building, the garden that surrounds it and the *roji* (ritual approach route) are significant: all are inspired by a rule with the surprising definition of, in essence, the tendancy to impede all rules.

Architectural Renovation
Discussion on architectural "renovation" involves two different, but interrelated meanings of the term. There is renovation as attainment of a new condition, especially in the cultural sense, and as "renewal," as in partial or total substitution, even repetitively.

Let us start with the first meaning. There has been much and continuous discussion on the crises seen in Japan at the time of the Meiji restoration and, particularly, in the first decades of the 20th century when its architectural culture made real contact with that from the West. Significantly, it was in those years when the definition of the term "architecture" itself underwent an interesting, parallel event.

"Western ideas on architecture are completely incongruous to the Japanese mentality; there is not even an equivalent word to 'architecture', which refers to all buildings of at least some artistic merit. In the traditional language there is the term *Zoka*, which relates to the construction of houses, and *Fushin*, which refers to the collection of funds for the construction or reconstruction of temples, but these cannot be generalized, being inseparable from their respective ritual modalities. So a new term, equivalent to the Western 'architecture' was coined: *Kenchiku*. The intention was that it should primarily indicate the artistic merit of buildings, but in common usage—as contemporary scholar Shinji Koike relates—the term is used mainly to indicate the entirety of technical operations in the construction sphere. This shows how the Japanese concept differs from the Western one, not just in scope but also in its mental framework. Europeans, following the Renaissance view, think of an abstract, general value which regards just one aspect of building activity; the Japanese, like medieval men, think of a concrete, particular activity, whose various aspects are perceived globally and unitarily."[14]

After World War II, a very difficult time for the country's social psychology, Japanese architects started their battle to gain international recognition and legitimacy. As has been said, they swiftly learned that if, on the one hand, they needed to appear competitive on the themes by which the debate was measured in the West, on the other, they also needed to demonstrate an autonomous, original identity, one in continuity with their traditional values. Some of these values in particular are of great interest.

The first is tied to the sense of the cyclical that impregnates every aspect of life. It derives from the turn of the seasons, which are quite distinct in Japan, but also, more generally, from the sense of cosmic cycling, which allows, for example, for the periodic reconstruction of temples (constructed of wood, and hence subject to a certain deterioration).

This brings us to the second meaning of renovation. Since the 8th century, the sanctuary of Ise has been completely reconstructed every twenty years or so. The process underwent just one unexpected interruption, lasting around 120 years before some regularity returned. The pause came in 1467, at the start of the Ōnin wars, during the Sengoku (literally "belligerent states") period. The next reconstruction should take place in the fall of 2014. Hence what we actually see "is not a real entity that has existed since the Nara period, but a faithful reproduction of the original, timeless beauty of a structure still full of life. Western stone structures, like the Parthenon or the pyramids, are different: we regard them today like well-preserved ruins. At the Iso sanctuary, the expression and spirit of the architecture is preserved rather than its physical entity."[15] And if what we have before us does not live up to our expectations, we must not forget that "the *oku*, the invisible center of things, is none other than the concept of convergence towards zero."[16] The disillusionment may not only occur to a Westerner's eye: "When I was

Traditional house,
Shinagawa-ku

young," recalls Fumihiko Maki, "I was taken to see the Meiji sanctuary, or that of Ise, and when we finally arrived I was disappointed by the total nullity of the objects of worship."[17]

Reconstruction as a purification rite was carried out regularly during the feudal period, in different places and in different ways, and is regarded as a clear rule of the Shintō cult. This is also manifestly linked with the concept of building maintenance, which is regarded with the same sort of attitude that we might apply to boats, one requiring the periodic, continuous substitution of new parts for old ones. Wooden buildings, especially religious ones, generally require careful cleaning daily; a series of seasonal adaptations such as the positioning or removal of screens and closures; the annual substitution of the paper in the sliding *shoji* screens; the reconstruction of the *tatami* mats (created for the size of a human being's vital space, 182 by 91 centimeters, except in Kansai where the length reaches 197 centimeters) around which the various rooms are planned, of the *fusuma* panels every few years; the rebuilding of the roof every fifty years or so; and the complete reconstruction of the internal building every 300 years. Similar behavior is now naturally directed towards contemporary buildings in which, however high-tech they may be, it is not difficult to find traditional aspects. The anxiety about such renewal is noticeable and clearly present everywhere: a Japanese law demands the reconstruction of public buildings every thirty years or so.[18]

Architectural Spaces and Surfaces

The role played by the horizontal surfaces on which people tread is significant in the correct understanding of the city of Tokyo and its architecture. This obliges us to return to the difficult concept of *oku*, earlier roughly defined as the "invisible center of things" or "convergence towards zero."

As Maki again notes, "*Oku* enhances horizontality and finds its symbolism in an invisible depth," a horizontality destined to become one of the cornerstones of Wrightian poetics.[19] The importance attached to it is obvious if you think about the habit, still universally applied, of removing one's shoes on entering a house, or any other space attributed particular dignity. Indeed, the interior of the home belongs to a higher spatial order. Unlike in the West, most of the attention of users of architectural space is dedicated to horizontal surfaces. Their use is never determined unambiguously: the same space can be used for sleeping, eating or receiving guests, and each of these functions may flow easily into the next. In traditional houses, floors are raised to protect them from ground humidity and to provide better ventilation. Ceilings are generally lower than in the West, even more so in older buildings. The horizontal perspective of an average user of an internal space is always low, at the height of a man seated cross-legged on the ground in the position of meditation; cushions and mattresses are arranged casually, directly on the *tatami* mats that soften the floors, ready to be removed and stored when not in use. Even traditional doors are often considered low by Western standards. The ancient access points to tea ceremony houses, which are only sixty centimeters high represent the extreme cases: they are little more than holes into which to crawl on all fours.

The internal space in Japanese architecture, especially the domestic space, is permeated by the concept of *oku*. Maki observes that "it is obvious when the various forms of development in living modes in Japan are studied that *oku* has a definitive status in our society. . . . Before World War II there were many houses in our city that, aside from variations to the layout, generally contained a room for receiving guests, a room for family members and often a more internal room (*okuzakishi*) for entertaining special guests or for the use of the head of the household, a room that often had an altar in one corner. The *okuzakishi* is on one hand very private but, on the other, becomes public in a ceremonial sense."[20]

Maki offers us the most profound definition of the concept: "After having visited many foreign cities I discovered that these multiple layers exist only in Japan. It is one of the most characteristic and rare of phenomena. It seems to me that the Japanese have always imagined the notion called *oku* (the most internal space) in the heart of these dense, multi-stratified, spatial formations, which I would compare to an onion. The expression *oku* is part of our daily spatial living; it indicates a notion of position in space—a sense of place—that only the Japanese possess. It is interesting to note that the word *oku*, when used in reference to spatial matters, always infers the concept of *okuyuki* (depth), which indicates a relative distance or an impression of distance in a given space. Compared with other peoples, the Japanese have lived in com-

munities of relatively high density since ancient times and therefore have developed a sense of finite, intimate space. One would think that a delicate sensitivity to the arrangement of the relative differences in distance within limited spaces has existed in the Japanese spirit since time immemorial. At the same time, the term *oku* implies something abstract and profound. It is an esoteric concept, and it is also used to express psychological depth, a sort of spiritual *oku*."[21] Carl Gustav Jung had no doubt of the "natural" capacity for psychological introspection in the Japanese consciousness when he wrote in 1928, "What we consider to be a specific discovery of the West, i.e. psychoanalysis and the various movements instigated by it, looks like the attempts of beginners compared with the proficiency that the Orientals had already reached in this field a very long time ago."[22]

The home is not a shelter but a filter, an open structure, permeable to nature, which is linked organically and intimately to it: the internal parts are almost external parts and vice versa; the gardens and their reflections of water find their *raison d'être* in immediate, direct contact with the building; the contemplation of seasonal cycles is the primary function of domestic architecture; its asymmetric, simple geometries—Wrightian *ante litteram*—form an indispensable counterpoint to the complex anarchy of the animal, vegetable and mineral worlds, to the search for sophisticated eurhythmy, for never-ending harmonies. It is the deep emotion inherent in the concept of *mono no aware*, the "aesthetic sensitivity for things."

"The room preserves its prescribed limits, the mats on the floor, the flat windows, the bamboo-covered walls (the pure image of the surface), into which the sliding doors merge: everything here is treated as if the room had been composed by a single touch of a brush. Nevertheless, on second impressions, this rigor becomes elusive. The inner walls are fragile, breakable, the outer walls slide, the furniture folds, so that in

the Japanese room one discovers that 'imagination' (in furnishings) through which every Japanese evades the conformism of its frame, without the trouble or the act of undermining it."[23] "In the corridor, as in the ideal Japanese house, without furniture (or with rarefied furnishing) there is no spot that designates even minimal ownership, no seat, bed or table from which the body can appoint itself as the subject (or master) of a space: the center is relinquished (burning frustration for a Western man, everywhere provided with his armchair, his bed, owner of a domestic *position*)."[24]

An archaic, monastic rigor seems to pervade the various domestic environments: "Even in the richest houses the supreme rule is economy: every aspect of domestic life is marked by maximum simplicity."[25] There is never anything superfluous; all objects are carefully hidden from view when not in use. Works of art are exhibited in the *tokonoma*, a specially created niche, but never all together: they are cycled, a few at a time, according to traditional rules of taste that enhance their individual presence in exemplary manner.

Traditional houses also have large projecting roofs. Bruno Taut relates this to the mutability of the seasons: "The highly protruding roofs have the double function of protecting the inside from rain and shielding it from the sky's excessive brightness, at the same time inducing one to look downwards, towards the ground and the vegetation."[26] The pronounced overhangs guarantee large areas of shade. The shadows and their variation with the seasons and weather conditions form the only indirect decoration on the internal walls, invariably painted the lightest shade of gray. They are an expression of that "hidden order" of which Yoshinobu Ashihara spoke, poles apart from clarity, strength and rationality, from those ideas of architectonic perfection underlying Western history from Ancient Greece to Rome, the Renaissance and the modern movement.[27]

Shadows in particular are poetically perceived as the origin of the "colors of darkness": "Have you ever seen, you who are reading this, the true darkness illuminated by a candle flame? Don't believe that it is like any other darkness, for instance that which surrounds you when you walk along the street at night. The darkness I am talking about is a sort of faint, ash-gray, fine dust and each of its particles seems to glow with all the colors of the rainbow."[28] Alternatively they are seen as antithetical, complementary aspects of the visual dynamic in things: "Light and shade are the two opposite sides of the same thing: the place illuminated by sun is always reached from the deepest shade, and the most intense joy is sadness; the greater the pleasure the more acute the suffering. If you try to separate them you lose yourself. If you try to eliminate them the world collapses."[29]

Nature and Catastrophe

As in California, the Japanese spirit is strongly permeated by natural catastrophes. This is reflected in the architecture, with the need for anti-seismic constructions that will also resist flood and the strong oceanic winds, but also in the constant sense of precariousness that pervades everything that is built. The "emergency culture" and the obsession for safety, as in all wealthy countries, are omnipresent and are felt through a whole series of details, starting with the obligatory torches on the bedside tables of every hotel room.

Traditional architecture is deeply, intimately permeated by it. Rob Mallet-Stevens pertinently wrote in 1911: "No Nippon construction has foundations because these could sway too easily. Buildings are set on wooden supports, simply placed on stone plinths; this gives the whole thing great elasticity and also allows water drainage beneath the floors without touching them. . . . In the constant expectation of earthquakes, the houses are built of wood and have just one floor. Glass doors or windows, which would be dangerous in the event of a quake, have been replaced by translucent paper on light frames."[30] But here again there is more: it is the Japanese will to respond, with cold, scientific efficiency, to unpredictable events and to engage in a dialogue with nature, which, as extraordinarily beautiful as it is, can sometimes be perilously treacherous. "We Japanese," writes Akio Morita, "are obsessed with survival. . . . We live our daily lives on these volcanic islands with the constant threat not only of a destructive earthquake but typhoons, tidal waves, blizzards and spring floods. Water aside, our islands do not supply us with raw materials and less than a quarter of our land is inhabitable or cultivable. This is why we consider everything we have to be precious. And this is why we have learned to respect nature, preserve it, miniaturize it, and to look on technology as a way to help us survive."[31]

If there is one aspect of Japanese tradition that still, despite everything, is safe from the contemporary megalopolis, it is its greenery. Unexpectedly, given what emerges from even a superficial visit, Tokyo is a city marked by marvelous parks and gardens, from those surrounding the Imperial Palace right down to the last patch of private green. In areas that are more than densely urbanized, often irreversibly devastated

Moat of the Imperial Palace, Chioda-ku

Terraced paddy fields

Rob Mallet-Stevens,
traditional buildings, from
L'architecture au Japon,
1911

by an invasive infrastructure, and where it would seem that not even a blade of grass could grow, you will be surprised to find that a large number of public and, especially, private gardens can readily be found, forming real oases of tranquility, often hidden behind discreet walls.

Japanese landscape culture merits a book all to itself; the refinement of its green areas and the care taken in planning and maintaining them is without equal in the West, with the possible exception of Great Britain. But here, more than anywhere else, a garden is always so overtly full of so many meaningful symbolic connotations, so marked by historical stratifications, so tied to the philosophical and religious dimension of whoever uses it, that it goes well beyond anything that we can imagine: "A tree, a rock, a waterfall become full of meaning, in that in themselves you can sense the divine nature that fills not just man's spirit but also his body."[32]

Such an exhaustive aesthetic sensibility to artificial nature has ancient origins. In the grandiose *Story of Genji (Genji monogatari)*, a literary masterpiece written by Murasaki, a lady who lived in the court of the emperor Ichijō around the year 1000, we find the words: "Genji planted a flower border with cinquefoil, red damsons, cherries, kerria, mountain azaleas and other plants that thrive in spring; because he knew that Murasaki [another character in the book] had a particular passion for the spring. . . . The garden of Akikonomu was full of the trees that take on their deepest hues in fall. The stream above the waterfall was drained and made to flow deep at a considerable distance; and so that the noise of the fall could reach further, Genji placed great boulders in the middle of its bed against which the current broke."[33]

The garden is the expression of *mono no aware*, man in tune with nature, and at the same time the supreme representation of nature itself. It must have no trace of artificial elements. This, naturally, makes it extremely artificial, but it doesn't matter, the garden is the representation of an abstract, idealized nature, a sort of figuration of original earthly paradise or the pre-figuration of heavenly paradise. Tellingly, it must appear *sabi*, as old as possible, which means ancient trees and moss-covered stones, which are corroded by time, water, etc. Water, in all its forms is the essential, indispensable element: as a pond, a lake, a stream or a waterfall. If possible you should be able to see its origin, whether from a waterfall or a spring, and this latter should be to the left of the main field of vision so that the water flows to the right. This is in homage to ancient Chinese beliefs but also to aesthetic-psychological considerations. The shape of whatever contains it, be it a pond, a lake or something else, should be as irregular as possible. Lakes will have peninsulas and islets, perhaps covered with dwarf pines or other small plants, which from a distance help to make them appear larger than they are. The rocks that surround the water or punctuate the green areas are usually of local origin and are arranged according to three different criteria: *ishigumi* (artificial), Chinese taste, and the expressively named *sute-ishi* (abandoned stones). Wooden bridges are important elements in the dynamic of walkways.

The role played by plants is also obviously fundamental. The principal place goes to evergreen trees; these alternate with deciduous plants, which are particularly appreciated for their recurrence with the seasonal cycles, their spring flowering and the spectacle their dead leaves offer

Katsuhiro Miyamoto,
installation of the Japanese
pavilion, Venice Biennial,
1996

Garden

in fall. Lawns are normally avoided. Instead open spaces are filled with moss, if in the shade, or avenues of low bushes and dwarf plants.

The gardens destined for *cha-no-yū*, the tea ceremony, are poetic and meaningful, even more so those inspired by the school of Zen, planned on criteria of absolute simplicity so as to generate serenity in their guests: "Where Zen is distinguished from other schools is in the firm negation of any faith in intellect. Salvation and illumination come suddenly, they explode in intuition. The garden is therefore one of the most delightful points where the I and the not-I can dissolve and sublimate, like the mixing of the waters of river and ocean. The garden is more important than treatises, syllogisms, or ancient writings. It is the song of things. Hence designing gardens was work undertaken with reverent commitment by the greatest minds of the Far East."[34]

The ancient respect for nature is also at the center of contemporary architectural sensibility. Even if Japan's political decisions of the recent past have not always been shared by European ecological culture, and its urbanistic and architectural decisions have been rather indifferent, not to say aggressive, in relation to nature (Tokyo, contradicting what has been said above, is also one of the least "natural" cities imaginable), there is no architect who today does not profess great attention to the landscape in which he is commissioned to work.

Tadao Ando, one of the most sensitive and, in many ways, one of the most critical of the cultural inclinations of the West, does not hesitate to declare in elegiac tones his respectful love for nature: "When I was young we often used to go to Kyoto or Nara to wander among the ancient architecture and I grasped the essence of Japanese architecture as inseparable from nature. . . . Far from the characteristic Western vision of nature as something to subdue and curb, the Japanese realized that they were part of it, and from their love and understanding of nature they made it their ideal to act in harmony with it. This difference is obviously reflected in the architecture. . . . There results a fluid exchange between inside and outside; if you analyze the traditional Japanese habitation, you invariably reach a point where it dissolves into nature. All the materials come from the surrounding environment and it is difficult to decide where man's artifice begins and ends. Simple and spontaneous, Japanese architecture melds with nature, while Western architecture is structural; it sets itself

121

opposite nature and is independent of what surrounds it. . . . . The recognition—enclosed within the *shizenkan* or 'vision of nature', of oriental philosophy—that humanity and nature are in reality just one thing, is still passed down and firmly preserved in the spirit of the Japanese."[35]

All this is true, alive, and present in the creativity of every architect. It would nevertheless be a mistake to place too much importance on the role that these traditional aspects play in contemporary planning. If the past is undoubtedly part of the Japanese collective psychology, it is perhaps configured (especially in Tokyo and quite unlike what happens in Italy, for example) rather like something similar to an abstract mental state that cannot and must not slow down the unstoppable, uncritical, vertiginous rush towards the new. We find evidence of this in the detached observations of Kazuyo Sejima: "I never consider traditional architecture to be an entity or model against which to match myself. I have it in my blood and it acts within me and in my planning without my being aware of it; however I think it is Westerners who analyze Japanese architecture in these terms rather than the Japanese themselves."[36]

[1] Cf. D. Libeskind, interviewed by L.Sacchi, in *Il Progetto*, no. 3, 1998.

[2] Cf. H. Suzuki, "Japanese Architecture Today," edited by Y. Futagawa, in *GA Document Japan '96*. Tokyo: 1996.

[3] B. Taut, "Architecture nouvelle au Japon," in *L'Architecture d'aujourd'hui*, no. 334, November 2001. The original manuscript, written in German, is preserved at the Iwanami Publishing House in Tokyo.

[4] Quoted in P. Riani, *Kenzo Tange*. Florence: Sansoni, 1977, p. 19.

[5] Cf. G. Bakaert, R. de Meyer, *A Journey to Japan, Where Chance Is the Standard*. Ghent: Ghent University Architectural and Engineering Press, 2001, pp. 26-27.

[6] C. Baglioni, "Quattro passi nel contesto," in *Casabella*, no. 608-609, 1994.

[7] R. Barthes, *L'Empire des signes*. Geneva: Skira, 1970.

[8] G. Bekaert, R. de Meyer, op. cit., p. 13.

[9] R. Barthes, op. cit.

[10] Ibid., p. 87.

[11] G.C. Calza, *Stile Giappone*. Turin: Einaudi, 2002, p.12.

[12] Ibid., p. 13.

[13] B. Taut, *Fundamentals of Japanese Architecture*. Tokyo: Kokusai Bunka Shinkokai, 1936, pp. 10-11.

[14] L. Benevolo, *Storia dell'architettura moderna*. Rome-Bari: Laterza, 1973, p. 831. Cf. S. Kolke, *Contemporary Architecture in Japan*. Tokyo: Shokokusha Pub. Co., 1953, p. 16.

[15] Y. Ashihara, *The Hidden Order, Tokyo through the Twentieth Century*. Tokyo-New York: Kodansha International, 1989, pp. 121-122. Originally published in Tokyo in 1986.

[16] F. Maki, "Japanese City Spaces and the Concept of Oku," in *The Japan Architect*, May 1979.

[17] Ibid.

[18] Cf. *Saper credere in architettura, Ventinove domande a Kazuyo Sejima, Ryue Nishizawa*, edited by L. Spita. Naples: Clean, 2003, p. 38.

[19] F. Maki, op. cit.

[20] Ibid.

[21] Ibid.

[22] C.G. Jung, *Il problema dell'inconscio nella psicologia moderna* (1928), quoted in G.C. Calza, op. cit., p. 41.

[23] R. Barthes, op. cit.

[24] Ibid.

[25] B. Taut, "Architettura nuova in Giappone," in *Casabella*, no. 676, 2000.

[26] Ibid.

[27] Cf. Y. Ashihara, op. cit.

[28] J. Tanizaki, "In'ei raisan" [In praise of shadows], in *Keizai Orai*, December 1933 and January 1934.

[29] S. Natsume, *Kusamakura* [The grass pillow]. Tokyo: 1906.

[30] R. Mallet-Stevens, "L'architecture au Japon," in *La Revue*, May 1911.

[31] A. Morita, *Made in Japan, Akio Morita and Sony*. New York: Weatherhill, 1987.

[32] G.C. Calza, op. cit., p. 44.

[33] S. Murasaki, *Genji monogatari* [The tale of Genji], trans. by E. Seiden-Sticker. London: Penguin Books, 1981.

[34] F. Maraini, *Ore Giapponesi*. Bari: Leonardo da Vinci Editrice, 1957.

[35] T. Ando, *East and West, Orient, Occident: Einflu? auf Design und Architektur*, ed. W. Blaser. Düsseldorf: Beton-Verlag, 1991.

[36] K. Sejima in *Saper credere in architettura*, op. cit., p. 48-49.

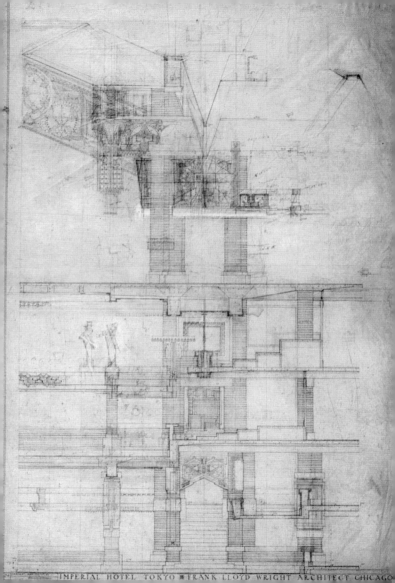

IMPERIAL HOTEL TOKYO ■ FRANK LLOYD WRIGHT ARCHITECT CHICAGO

5. The Presence of Masters

The westernization and modernization of Tokyo's urban structure and architecture, an ongoing development process since the end of the 19th century, are largely ascribable to the influence of three prominent foreign planners, particularly in the first half of the 20th century. These masters of modernity are associated with different periods of Japanese history: Frank Lloyd Wright went to Japan in the early 1900s, Bruno Taut in the thirties and Le Corbusier in the 1950s. Some minor figures should also be mentioned, notably the Japanese Arata Endō, a Wright pupil, and the Czech Antonin Raymond, who went to Japan with Wright, but will end up playing a pivotal role, as we shall later see, between the inheritance of the American master and Le Corbusier.

Frank Lloyd Wright

As mentioned above Wright first went to Tokyo in 1905. In his book *The Japanese Print* (1912) he highly praises Japanese prints, works that will greatly influence his later architectural design style. In 1914 his Taliesin buildings burned down, with the well-known, dramatic implications for the architect's private and professional life.

Frank Lloyd Wright,
Imperial Hotel 1912-23
Partial section

Frank Lloyd Wright,
Imperial Hotel 1912-23
(demolished in 1968)

Frank Lloyd Wright,
Odawara Hotel, Nagoya,
1917

The celebrated studio-home was gradually reconstructed and its plan certainly recalls the imperial villa of Katsura, near Kyōto, built with the supervision of the theosophist Kobori Enshō in the early 17th century, a sublime, abstract *summa* of classic Japanese architecture and garden art.

In the immediate post-war period, between 1918 and 1922, Wright spent nearly all his time in Tokyo, held by the Imperial Hotel contract. The Hollyhock House was then being built in Los Angeles and the long absence of the architect caused continuous conflicts with his Californian client Aline Barnsdall, an eccentric millionaire fascinated by Marxism. Wright sent therefore to the site one of his best Taliesin assistants, the young Rudolph Schindler, then little over thirty.

The Imperial Hotel was Wright's first major Japanese assignment and kept him busy for a long time, from 1912 to 1923. It was a huge, oriental-style, mannered edifice, with classical symmetrical structure and foundations predating the mushroom column solution adopted for the Johnson Wax headquarters. This enabled the building to withstand, suffering very little damage, the 1923 earthquake. In 1957 Wright wrote in his autobiography, *A Testament*, "The Imperial Hotel, built for the royal household of Japan, was a tribute to Japan as she was rising from her knees to her feet. She had been eating from the floor, sleeping on the floor, and now had to learn to sit at tables and climb into bed to sleep. The building was intended to harmonize with those around the moat across the park before it. The royal household was shocked when I decided to use Oya, the stone-ordinaire under foot in Tokyo for the structure, with a brick handmade in Japan for the first time. The architect persevered, finally got what he wanted, and great blocks of Oya began floating down by sea and canal from the quarries of Nikko to the site. But a permit to build the building was awaited in vain. Finally a meeting with the authorities was held at which they took the view that a world famous architect would not come to Japan to build something that would fall down under any circumstances. They could not understand the

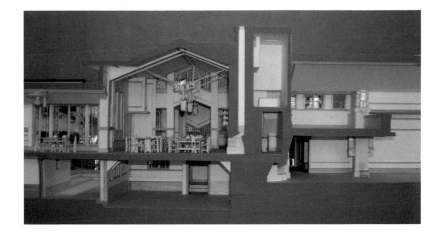

propositions we made but were willing to watch and wait and probably learn something worth learning. Accordingly we proceeded—to build the building with all the help they could give. I have sometimes been asked why I did not make the opus more 'modern.' The answer is that there was a tradition there worthy of respect and I felt it my duty as well as my privilege to make the building belong to them so far as I might. The principle of flexibility instead of rigidity here vindicated itself with inspiring results. But the A.I.A. commission sent to study conditions in Japan subsequent to the great temblor of 1922 made no mention of the structure".[1]

In the same period Wright also designed the Odawara Hotel in Nagoya (1917) and made the preliminary plan for a villa at Ashiya, on the Rokko Mountain, not far from Kōbe. This was an orientalized version of the Californian residences of the time—from the already mentioned Hollyhock (1916-1921) to Millard, the so-called Pasadena "Miniature" (1923)—with a special emphasis on the qualities of the Japanese home spaces. Built in 1924, the house has recently been accurately restored by the current owners, the Jodogawa Steel Company, who use it as a guest house.

The Jiyū Gakuen girls' school in Mejiro was built by Wright in 1921, with the assistance of Arata Endō, a student at Taliesin in 1917 and assistant at the Imperial Hotel site in 1919. In particular, Endō designed the school's auditorium, which was completed independently in 1934, on the opposite site of the road. The institute's founders, Yoshikazu and Motoko Hani, a married couple who met Wright through Endō, aimed at building an experimental school inspired by *laissez-faire* principles; "Jiyū Gakuen" means "School of Freedom".

In time the school grew and a boys' section was added. It was then decided to move it to a new campus in Minamisawa. The original buildings were renamed Myōnichikan, that is "House of Tomorrow" and were used by the ex-pupils for cultural activities and various other purposes. At the end of the 1990s the estate—an independent, perfectly self-contained and elegant structure with an unusually symmetrical C-plan set around a large open courtyard—underwent careful restoration with new, small, service additions. The bright interiors, all furnished with original items, still offer a peaceful atmosphere and pleasant flowing spaces.

Wright was to relate at length his enthusiastic appreciation of Japanese culture in *An Autobiography*, published in 1932, particularly on the subject of prints: "During the last years passed in the Oak Park Workshop, Japanese prints had attracted me and I had learned a great deal from them. The elimination of the insignificant and the process of sim-

Frank Lloyd Wright,
Jiyū Gakuen 1921, Interior

Frank Lloyd Wright,
Jiyū Gakuen 1921, Interior

Frank Lloyd Wright,
Jiyū Gakuen 1921

plification in which I was already involved was endorsed by them. And once I discovered the beauty of its prints, Japan continued to exert a strong pull on me. Later I became aware that Japanese art and architecture had a truly organic character. The art of the Japanese was closer to the earth, it was a more autonomous product of more indigenous conditions of life and work, so in my opinion it came far closer to the modern than the art from any other European or faded civilization."[2]

Endō (1889-1951) designed some remarkably interesting buildings, clearly influenced by the master, such as the Kondō villa at Fujisawa, in the Kanagawa prefecture. Originally built in 1925 in the Tsujidō woods, then rebuilt in its current location, this is a two-story house characterized by a balloon frame structure and a western-style framework, focused around a central fireplace, though also including traditional rooms with tatami on the floors. The very low ceilings belong both to the typical style of the American master and to the Japanese residential tradition.

Frank Lloyd Wright's influence is also detectable in other buildings: a significant example are the exteriors of the United Church of Christ in Takanawa, built by Takehiko Okami in 1932. Okami had moved to Taliesin in 1928. Four years later he opened his studio in Tokyo and, at a time when growing Japanese nationalism was causing serious difficulties to the Christian communities, gained his first commission from a group of Protestant churches united under a single denomination.

In 1919 Wright brought to Japan Antonin Raymond (1890-1976), a Czech architect who had already had the Japanese Kunio Maekawa in his own studio team. Raymond had collaborated with the master on the Imperial Hotel project, but gradually grew apart from what he defined as Wrightian "mannerism," decidedly shifting towards the European Modern Movement and the Corbusian brutalism in particular. In 1923 he built his own house in Reinanzaka, adopting the International Style and this is rightly considered the breakpoint with his cumbersome Wrightian inheritance. Three years later he built in Yokohama a more conventional villa for the Swiss businessman Ehrismann. Demolished in 1982, to make way for a condominium, it was reconstructed in a nearby park in 1990 and later opened to the public.

The same municipality of Naka, in Yokohama, also hosts the Ferris University #10 building, designed in 1929 to provide accommodation for the Rising Sun Petroleum company staff. It was built in reinforced concrete, with essential white parallelepiped volumes and large rectangular windows.

In 1932 the American J. Bergamini completed the chapel of St. Luke's International Hospital in Chuo on the basis of a design by Raymond. As in other Christian churches of the same period, the gothic style prevailed at St. Luke, and it may be hypothesized that the questionable stylistic criteria imposed by the client induced Raymond to abandon the job. Another Czech, the engineer Jan Svagr, worked in the S. Luke's team in these years. He then built in 1933 another neo-gothic church, the Sacred Heart in Yokohama, elevated to the rank of cathedral with the town achieving a diocesan status in 1937.

Bruno Taut

Taut reached Japan by sea on May 3rd 1933, together with his partner Erica Wittich, having crossed the Soviet Union from Moscow to Vladivostok. A Japanese professor, K. Imai, had already been in contact with him, as well as with Gropius, Mies van der Rohe and Le Corbusier. In an open letter to his Japanese colleagues, probably written in Switzerland in March 1933 and entitled *Zu meiner bevorstenhenden Reise nach*

Bruno Taut, *House of a priest at Sendai*, 1933

Bruno Taut, *Camellias in the snow*, 1934

Japan ("On My Imminent Journey to Japan"), Taut clearly acknowledges how much the West owes to this Eastern country, not so much for its exotic components, but rather for its indirect endorsement of modern architectural theories, its natural simplicity and the significance bestowed on the concept of "emptiness."[3] The invitation to Japan was extended by Isaburo Ueno, spokesman for the Japanese Association for International Architecture. Taut had probably planned to stay about three months and to give a series of lectures, while waiting the outcome of his Moscow projects. Maybe he had in mind to go on to the United States, but in fact he stayed for three and a half years. As we know, he then ended up in Turkey, where he designed and built a series of buildings for the Ministry of Culture, dying on Christmas Eve of 1938.

On his arrival in Japan, Taut enthusiastically wrote in his travel journal: "Color! Green! Such color! Never seen before. Water with the colors of the iris, new world, . . . Cleanliness. . . . Enchanting!"[4] On May 4th, 1933, the day of his fifty-third birthday and just twenty-four hours since his arrival, he went to the imperial villa in Katsura. Moved and overcome by emotion, he wrote in a syncopated and highly poetic style: "A pure, unadorned architecture. Moving, innocent as a child. Realization of a modern desire. . . . Bamboo walkways, park!! Moon Court! Impression of beauty to the point of tears. . . . Infinitely impressive immediately so, for the wealth of the references. . . . A non-individual edifice, everything equal. . . . Total richness of the procedure in the interior, splendour in the waiting rooms, no splendour in the living spaces. Very refined differentiation of artistic pleasure. . . . Beauty for the eye: eye = that which transforms into the spiritual. This is Japan beauty at first glance."[5]

Almost exactly one year later Taut returned to Katsura and made twenty-eight analytical brush drawings in which all the principles of the new architecture, expressed in *Die neue Baukunst* (1929), can be found. From then on Katsura became a legendary ideal to both Westerners and Japanese, the absolute parameter for evaluating architectural quality, a "universal architecture." And from then on Taut became so enthusiastic about the Japanese architectural culture, and about this sublime example in particular, that maybe unconsciously he went as far as supporting "that which he abhorred more than anything: the contemporary Japanese militarism and its ideological bases, tendencies that led to the institution of what became known as the Berlin-Tokyo axis in the autumn of 1938."[6]

Much later Kenzō Tange, Toyo Ito and Arata Isozaki were to become deeply involved with Katsura. In the introduction to Tange's 1969 book, Walter Gropius wrote: "I am convinced that a scholar of art and architecture may draw invaluable benefits from a visit to Japan, where mature, sublime solutions to the complex spatial and human scale problems may be found: the true means through which the art of architectural creation is expressed."[7]

The many studies by Taut on the Japanese architecture and art are of great significance: *Nippon mit europäischen Augen gesehen*, a critical essay, was published in Tokyo in 1934 and caused considerable comments. In 1935 the *Grundlinien japanischer Architektur* was published and later translated into English under the title *Fundamentals of Japanese Architecture*. In 1936 *Japan Kunst* was published. Then, in 1937, *Das japanische Haus und sein Leben* appeared, again translated into English as *Houses and People of Japan*.

His ability to penetrate the Japanese compositional and constructional methods was extraordinary. The discrimination between the fleeting and the lasting issues, his reading of the sanctuary of Ise and the Katsura villa, his rejection of the pompous decorative apparatus of the Buddhist tradition, set against his appreciation of the austerity and simplicity of other wooden constructions—these are just some of the many topics he successfully handled, clearing the field of a number of ambiguities that would only have created problems to architects in their new rush towards modernity. But the significance of his lesson lies most of all in the indirect approval of the hypothesis that the modern movement and a large part of Japanese constructional tradition are, in many ways, perfectly compatible.

In his last years Raymond, who had been dismissed by Taut as "very active,"[8] designed the admired Reader's Digest headquarters (1952), subsequently replaced by the Nikken Sekkei's Palace Side Building in 1966 (where the "Corbusian" quality of the prior construction was somehow safeguarded). He also wrote a book, *An Autobiography* (1973) echoing, at least in its title, the celebrated autobiographical work of the disputed American master. But in our opinion the existence of Raymond should still be regarded as exemplary, particularly as it reflects a widespread appreciation of Wright's lesson in Japan. As a matter of fact, apart from

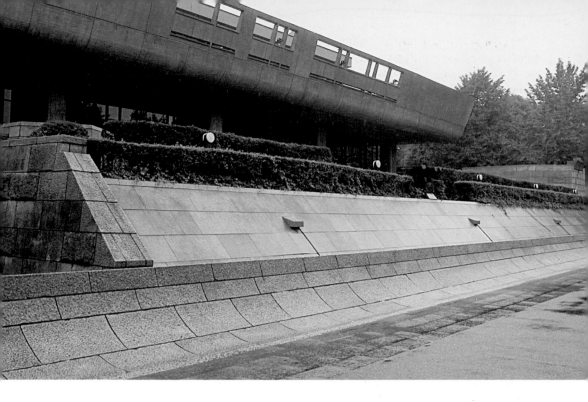

Le Corbusier, National Museum of Western Art, Ueno park, Taito-ku, 1957-59

the personal and often unproductive devotion of a number of disciples, his legacy would soon have been set aside in favor of a more or less un-conditional adhesion to the European rationalism and its American version by International Style. We might even say that the influence of the Japanese tradition on the work of Frank Lloyd Wright largely outper-forms that of Wright on Japanese architectural culture.

Le Corbusier
In this tale of complex exchanges between Japan and the West the cru-cial role is played by Le Corbusier, in the years following World War II. We owe just one great project to this Swiss master, that is the National Museum of Western Art. The commission, resulting from a strange com-bination of circumstances, came to him at a crucial time in his career, that of the post-war reconstruction period which had already permitted the realization of various "Unités d'habitation" which gave him consid-erable credit with the French government.

After the San Francisco peace treaty, signed in 1951, France resolved to return to shipowner Kōjirō Matsukata his valuable 19th and 20th-cen-tury collection of paintings and sculptures, mostly works by Impressionist masters, arbitrarily confiscated during the conflict. Matsukata had died a year earlier. The French government required the collection to be housed in a new museum devoted to Western art, explicitly indicating Le Corbusier as the architect.

133

Charlotte Perriand also went to Japan at that time. She wrote: "Tokyo 1956: modern buildings, small glass and cement fortresses, one after the other, housing the most unbelievable complexes: railway stations, metro, department stores, restaurants, theatres. At their feet a city of eight million inhabitants built from paper and wood . . . I imagine that I am returning to a Paris straight out of the Middle Ages, with all its ancient customs preserved, but embellished by modern buildings. Just imagine how this would be."⁹

Le Corbusier's museum, set in the Ueno park, was opened in 1959. The design was based on a square framework with a spiral winding around a central courtyard, without the traditional façades. This typology—the *musée à spirale carrée*—had been used experimentally in Ahmedabad in 1958 and was to be proposed again in Chandigarh in 1964. In theory, the spiral structure should have supported a limitless growth for the edifice as time went by, but none of the three museums ever grew as Le Corbusier had thought.

The project was supervised by three Japanese architects: Takamasa Yoshizaka, who had worked at Le Corbusier's Paris studio between 1950 and 1952, Kunio Maekawa (under whom Tange had been a pupil) and Junzō Sakakura, the latter two having worked with the master before the war.

Two new wings were later added, the New Wing by Maekawa, in 1979, and the Special Exhibition Gallery, much of it underground, in 1997, again by Maekawa, in collaboration with the technical office of the Ministry of Constructions. On both occurrences the original edifice, now designated the Main Building, lost much of its original coherence, but nevertheless the building's influence was enormous.

The rivalry between Wright and Le Corbusier seemed eventually to resolve over time in favor of the latter, at least on the Tokyo scene. Several determinant factors are clearly identifiable in this : first, the two masters belong to different generations and the opportunities available to Wright arose in a period when exchanges between the West and Japan were considered scarcely significant, while Le Corbusier's (only) opening was linked with the great season following the Second World War; second, the most important building designed by Wright, the Imperial Hotel, was unfortunately soon destroyed and the small school he built was obviously less renowned, while Le Corbusier's museum, though partially spoiled by several modifications, had a very strong impact on the public; third, the style-code proposed by Wright was soon dated and at the same time, highly personal, in fact too personal to be adopted creatively without being slavishly imitative, while the rationalist code of Corbusian derivation was easily transmittable by its very nature and was rapidly assimilated by the best young Japanese architects, led by Tange, becoming a real *lingua franca*.

Tafuri observed in this context: "The rationalist syntax offered a significant advantage, it immediately created a common platform allowing for the effective exchange of experiences in a movement that had become much more collective. Developing experiences once begun meant, first of all, a continuity with that common platform. To the Japanese Movement it already represented something of distinctive character and an inheritance to safeguard."[10]

In short, it does not seem excessive to state that a large part of the Tokyo's architecture of the 1960s and the 1970s stems more or less directly and recognizably just from the weighty Corbusian inheritance.

Le Corbusier, National Museum of Western Art, Ueno Park, Taito-ku, 1957-59

[1] F.Ll. Wright, *A Testament*. New York: Bramhall House, 1957 p. 123.
[2] F.Ll Wright, *Io e l'architettura*. Milan: 1955, p.304. Or. Ed. 1932.
[3] Cf. M. Speidel, "Bruno Taut 'Il mio punto di vista sull'architettura giapponese'," in *Casabella*, no. 676, 2000.
[4] Bruno Taut, in the manuscript preserved at the Iwanawi Publishing House, Tokyo. The Stiftung Archiv of the Akademie der Künste of Berlin, Abteilung Baukunst, owns a copy. Quoted in M. Speidel, op. cit.
[5] Ibid.
[6] M. Speidel, op. cit., n. 21. Remark by Heinrich Taut, in the foreword to the second edition of *Die Neue Baukunst*. Stuttgart: 1979, p. IX.
[7] W. Gropius, in K. Tange, *Katsura: Tradition and Creation in Japanese Architecture*. New Haven: Yale University Press, 1960.
[8] M. Spiedel, op. cit.
[9] Ch. Perriand, "Crisi del gusto in Giappone," in *Casabella*, no. 120, 1956.
[10] M. Tafuri, *L'architettura moderna in Giappone*. Bologna: Cappelli, 1964.

6. Contemporary Architecture

Today Tokyo is one of the great architectural capitals, possibly the most extraordinary capital of contemporary architecture in the world. Undoubtedly, this is due to the great experimental character of its creative scene in general and its architecture in particular, as well as to favorable economic conditions, especially throughout the 1980s and 1990s. But this condition was also brought about by unrestrictive building regulations, strong liberalism and the awareness that in any event, there is little to be gained by holding on to what already exists.

The city features buildings by all the major contemporary Japanese architects, from Kenzō Tange to Yoshinobu Ashihara, from Tadao Ando to Riken Yamamoto, from Fumihiko Maki to Arata Isozaki and Toyo Ito, from Kazuyo Sejima to Shigeru Ban. Thus, although a visit to Tokyo will not embrace the entire country's exceptional architectural wealth, it is certainly enough to give the Western observer a meaningful picture.

As explained earlier, the complexity and dimensions of the city's urban structure make it difficult to understand such a broad, multiform system. We will provide an initial, concise reference frame, on the assumption that, if it is true that Tokyo's contemporary architecture is— *tout court*—rightfully contemporary architecture, then our main concern is understanding its relationship with the city as a whole, but also, indirectly, the specifics of the Japanese situation on one side and its relations with the West on the other.

The Western Presence

As mentioned earlier, during the 1980s and 1990s the architectural scene was globalized. This was the time of Tokyo's unstoppable rise to its place as one of the greatest metropolises in the world. Those years saw the creative presence of a large number of celebrated European and American architects. Opening up the market had its drawbacks, and gave rise to criticism and resentment among the local architectural community. But those years were so full of commissions and work for everyone that such a process of internationalization became more feasible. "Naturally, in this country the architectural image is, more than anywhere else, a marketing tool, and this is the principal reason behind the many commissions awarded to the stars of Western architecture in Japan." Using foreign competence became "a neo-exotic component for the landscape of Japan's larger city."[1] It was almost as though the architectural scene were behaving like the fashion sector. Japanese clients were mostly attracted by the great international names, which acted as catalysts. This may be a part of a picture we have always had of Japan: the latest arrival in the Western salon, fiercely de-

Steven Holl, Makuhari
Bay-Town, Mihama-ku,
Chiba-ken, 1995
Tea room

termined to be accepted at the highest levels. But, as mentioned previously, Japan is an extraordinarily wealthy country, and pays great attention to planning and building quality. We ought to add that, on their part, Europeans and Americans "all are longing to build there, among the happy few—like Norman Foster or Philippe Starck. This is not only for money, which abounds all the same, but because it bestows a patina of consecration."[2]

Although at that time Japanese architectural culture was mature and full of high-level personalities, we believe that the liveliness and creativity of the current scene would hardly have reached such high levels without such an array of great names from America and Europe. The former include architects working for important studios, such as Cesar Pelli, Kevin Roche, Harry Weese, Hugh Stubbins, Kohn Pedersen Fox and Rafael Viñoly; but also refined designers such as Robert Venturi, Ricardo Legorreta, Peter Eisenman and Steven Holl. Among the Europeans, aside from the aforementioned Foster and Starck, there are Aldo Rossi, Mario Bellini, Paul Chemetov, Ricardo Bofill, Mario Botta, Renzo Piano, Richard Rogers, Branson Coates, David Chipperfield, Coop Himmelb(l)au, Jean Nouvel, Herzog & de Meuron and Foreign Office.

Giving a complete, yet concise picture of contemporary architectural activity would be beyond our scope. We shall limit ourselves to examples, indicating aspects of some of the more interesting typologies. Nevertheless, we must point out that countless high-quality examples are spread over a vast geographical area. In Tokyo, once more, figures are anything but insignificant.

The Home

Unsurprisingly, residential property is widespread and embraces a wide range of dimensions, from tiny, single-family homes to the world's most

extensive collective settlements. Along with religion, the housing sphere is where the attachment to tradition is strongest and most sensitive, and this is especially revealed in the distribution of the interiors. But, as the sector often constitutes the initial test for young architects, it is also marked by exceptional experimentalism, especially when dealing with small, single-family homes commissioned by cultured, sophisticated clients.

We must repeat that here we cannot carry out a comprehensive analysis of such a vast, multifaceted topic. Regrettably, extensive planning elements in the contemporary scene will not even be mentioned (such as, for instance, the often disquieting but nevertheless important public building projects in Tokyo's outskirts, which often assume record-breaking aspects, at least quantitatively). We shall, instead, restrict ourselves to discussing what is more easily accessible to the Western reader, both from a physical and a cultural point of view.

One notable example from the 1960s is the extensive residential complex of Hillside Terrace, by Fumihiko Maki. Built in stages over a period of almost 35 years (1969-92), it is sited along the Yamate-dōri, in an elegant area of Shibuya, and was commissioned by an important client, the Asakura family. A series of shopping centers and exhibition spaces also form part of this remarkably high-quality complex, as does the Danish embassy, which is finished in pink brickwork (1979), probably to distinguish it from the other buildings, at least colorwise.

The late 1970s and the early 1980s spawned a series of single-family houses that quickly raised their designers, all then very young, to international renown. In 1976, for example, came Kazuo Shinohara's house at Uehara: a "wild machine," as it was defined by the designer, para-

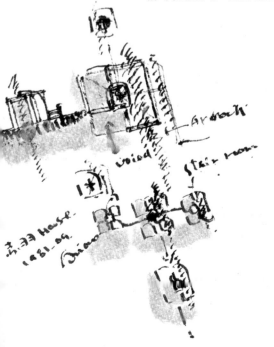

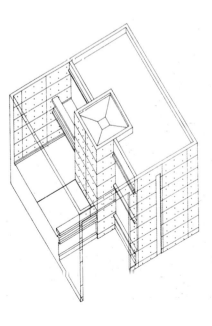

phrasing Claude Lévi-Strauss. The same year, Toyo Ito at Nakano designed a praiseworthy house on a horseshoe-shaped plan around a central courtyard, with a roof pitching toward the interior. This was followed by his Silver Hut in 1984, which was built in the same area; here he made extensive use of steel barrel-vaulting. Takefumi Aida was the author of the ten projects devoted to the Toy Block Houses, which often appeared in Postmodern reviews. Among these we will mention House III, in Nakano, (1981) and House X, in Shibuya, (1984). The whole series is characterized by the adoption of elementary volumes that look like children's building blocks. Furthermore, at least in the case of House III, primary colors enlivened the interior, while more sober grays and whites were used for the exterior. And here we come to Hiromi Fujii's Miyata house, built in 1980 for an editor-writer. This is more intellectual in conception, possibly influenced by the work Peter Eisenman was doing at the time. Based on an oblique grid, its interior is characterized by walls that appear deceptively like exterior façades.

Among the many large residential complexes, we will only mention the anonymous Ohkawabashi River City 21 on the Sumida river estuary, designed by the Tokyo Metropolitan Housing Supply Corporation. It has 3,100 apartments, built in stages from 1986 onwards, but we are referring to it only because it houses Toyo Ito's famous Egg of Winds (1991).

The egg forms part of a series of experiments carried out by Ito for a possible "floating" or "flying" residence envisaged for a single woman. The strange object does not actually function as such; it is more like a

Tadao Ando, Kidosaki house, 1985-86
Perspective drawing

Tadao Ando, Kidosaki house, 1985-86
Isometric projection

Tadao Ando, Fukuhara house, 1985-86
Isometric projection

Tadao Ando, Ito house, 1988-90
Isometric projection

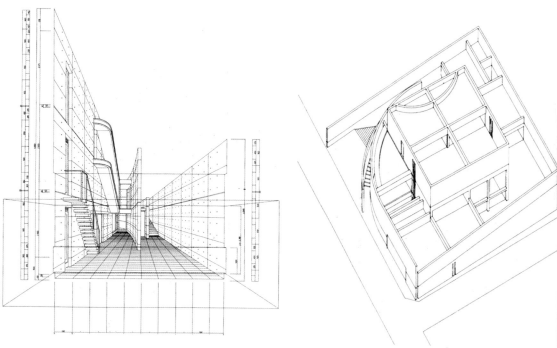

Tadao Ando, Building for
I Gallery housing,
Study draft

critical stance on the ephemeral nature of the contemporary city and its inhabitants. Its creator observed: "The residents of Tokyo can, I belive, be compared to nomads wandering in artificial forests. In housing complexes, no one stays at home during the day; even housewives go out. Most of the husbands only come home to sleep. . . . Today in Tokyo buildings are constructed and demolished at a bewildering speed. It is really stunning. Buildings invade the city and gain popularity, then, just as quickly, they are used up and discarded like a piece of paper. . . . Our ideas on semiology and superficiality are developing rapidly, but, even more rapidly, urban spaces have been metamorphosed into symbols and have become superficial."[3] The egg looks like a giant, aluminum rugby ball whose axes range from 16 to 8 meters. At night, five computers project different images onto five screens, producing an effect that picks up what was done in the architect's even more celebrated and ephemeral Tower of Winds, built in 1986 near Yokohama station.

Of greater interest is the Steven Holl quarter in Makuhari, in the Chiba prefecture (1992). Although it is smaller, it nevertheless constitutes an actual portion of the city, built with public financing, and, taken as a whole, forms one of the most interesting and balanced attempts at mediating between consolidated, modern housing styles and a subtle version of Japanese tradition (the use of water and greenery in the central courtyard, spaces devoted to the tea ceremony, etc.). The general plan features a square block housing 180 apartments with entrances at the four cardinal points. The simple design of the compositions is high-

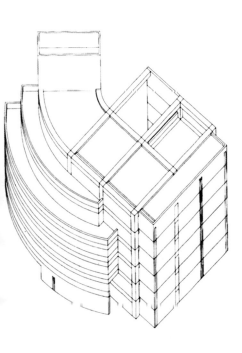

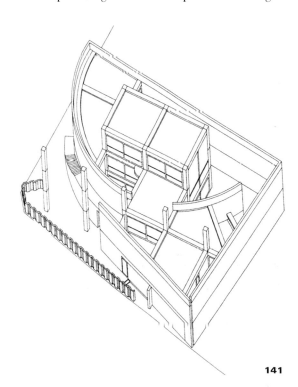

lighted by a series of slight architectural "dissonances" and a sequence of small individual elements: the "house of sun reflections," the "house of water reflections," the "house of color," the "house of azure shadows" and, especially, the "house of nothingness" which, from a roof terrace on one of the blocks, offers a view toward the bay and the sound of the ocean winds.

Many single-family houses have been built in Tokyo over the last few years, especially in the boundless outskirts; as mentioned earlier, they are often characterized by a high degree of experimentalism. Among these, we will point out the following: the tiny Truss Wall House by Eisaku Ushida and Kathryn Findlay at Machida-shi (1999), a NeoExpressionist, fluidly plastic, almost visceral dwelling, characterized by reinforced concrete walls molded on a ductile, net-like metallic structure; the house in Arakawa by Kei'ichi Irie + Power Unit Studio (2001), which has a minimalist feel, but makes creative use of color. Other examples are the house in Togoshi by Satoshi Okada (2002), entirely faced in galvanized iron, and Kengo Kuma's Plastic House (2002), built for the photographer Rowland Kirishima in the more central area of Meguro. Here, the architect explored the unpredictable potential and partial transparency of plastic materials.

With his expertise in the world of architecture, Shigeru Ban holds a special place in the sphere of one-family homes. He has now acquired international renown, after long experimentation in the wake of the best 20th century traditions, especially from America (from Mies van der Rohe to Neutra, Soriano, Saarinen, Ellwood and Eames, but also from John Hejduk to Richard Meier). His works include the Muramatsu house in Tokyo (1989), the Curtain Wall House in Itabashi-ku (1995), with its enormous draperies; and especially his small but interesting Glass Shutter House in Setagaya (2003). The latter, a building on three levels housing a restaurant on the second floor, features a sunshading device which disappears completely when it is not needed, as well as broad glazed areas, minimalist details and exclusive use of white. The colossal draperies are also white, drawing inspiration from his work in Itabashi, and adding sensuousness and softness to the rigid spatial warp of the very simple volume.

Buildings for Worship

Franco Purini once said that Tokyo proves that God does not exist. This is a credible thesis if you consider the city's chaotic conformation, its lack of any hierarchic structure, its unbridled consumerism, the impenetrability of its ethical and spiritual dimension—if such a dimension exists. There are few contemporary religious buildings in the city, and, from an architectural point of view, they are not very interesting. This is not only true for more recent constructions, but, generally speaking, for all of those that were built throughout the 20th century.

Take the clumsy Honganji temple in Tsukiji, by Chūta Ito (1934), for instance: an eclectic example of a Chinese, Indian, Javanese and Buddhist-Japanese Tenjika style from the Edo period. But not all examples are like that. Certainly, the Zenshoji temple at Taito, a work carried out in 1958 by Seiichi Shirai, is more interesting: a balanced, minimalist synthesis of the old and the new that shows respect for the traditional Buddhist style.

The spread of Christianity was fraught with difficulty, and was thus very limited. After World War II, it was seen as the religion of the American victors, which did not help it become more popular.

Things were different in Korea, for example, where the Americans were considered the liberators, and their religion saw immediate, huge success.

Therefore, relatively speaking, there are not many Christian churches in Tokyo. An exception which can be set in the climate of 19th century eclecticism is the Orthodox Church in Chiyoda-ku of 1891, designed by Josiah Conder on commission from the missionary Nikolai. This large building, which was based on a general plan by a Russian artist, was destroyed in the 1922 earthquake and was later rebuilt by Shin'ichiro Okada, who made some changes to the structure.

The Catholic cathedral of Saint Mary, which rises in a quiet neighborhood of Bunkyō-ku, is one of the most notable examples of contemporary religious buildings. Built by Kenzō Tange in 1964, after a competition a number of other renowned architects also took part in, including Yoshirō Taniguchi and Kunio Maekawa, it is distinguished by a cruciform

framework formed by four pairs of hyperbolic paraboloids (the highest two, at altar level, soar 40 meters). The structure, in ribbed reinforced concrete, is faced with very bright, slightly ribbed stainless steel on the exterior. Light filters through the long vertical glazing that separates the four pairs of surfaces. The passage of time and trends has not affected the materials, nor the image of the church. Now, forty years after it was planned, Tange's church is still very beautiful.

The Salesian Boys' Home in Kodaira-shi was built in 1988, a work by Sakakura Associates which includes an octagonal chapel revealing vigorous use of exposed face concrete.

Yet, a number of new, showy churches were built during the years of the Heisei Boom. This was not due to some sudden religious fervor (in a country where the Christian population still does not exceed 1%), but to the spread of a curious trend that is still fashionable today: people like marrying in church, according to the traditional Western rite. None of these are high-quality churches—in Tokyo at least—although they can be set in the sphere of curiosities. (Obviously, the case of the many famous Christian chapels designed by Tadao Ando in other parts of the country is different).

However, we have a remarkable example from 1995, Fumihiko Maki's Church of Christ, which rises along the Yamate-dōri, not far from the Hillside Terrace residential complex. It was built in concrete faced with bushhammered granite (cedar formworks were used) and glass (translucent, with fiberglass fitted between the various layers), and features refined wooden interiors. Adjacent spaces house the parish offices, waiting rooms, meeting rooms etc. The nave is enclosed by a lowered vault marked by built-in lights, and the side walls bend slightly upwards. The floor, in Finnish birch, whose hues resemble those of tatami mats, and the walls, which make use of glass and fiberglass that are similar to shojis, help bring the interior's rarefied atmosphere closer to that of traditional houses.

Also notable is the terse Ossuary by Shōzō Uchii, built in 1993 inside the old cemetery of Tama, which dates from 1923: a multistory complex marked by a subversive, upturned truncated cone shape.

Parks and Gardens

Much has been said of the extraordinary quality achieved by landscape architecture in Japan, and the multiple meanings ascribed to parks and gardens. Tokyo still offers a great number of beautiful, perfectly maintained and preserved historical examples. The Koishikawa Kōrakuen Gardens, for instance, are in the heart of Bunkyō-ku, not far from the Tokyo Dome and the Kanda river. It is a complex from the early Edo period, and its original nucleus, dating from 1629, was built for Tokugawa Yorifusa, a member of the Tokugawa dynasty's Mito branch.

But the contemporary scene is rich and multifaceted too. The most interesting works include: the War-Dead Memorial Park by Takefumi Aida, also in Bunkyō-ku (1988), built in tribute to the citizens who died during World War II; the Unerdaiichi Plaza, near Shimbashi station, by

Claes Oldenburg's saw in
the Seven Springs Park,
Expo Center, Teleport Town

Takefumi Aida, War-Dead
Memorial Park, Bunkyō-ku,
1988

Arc Crew (1999); Seven Springs, annexed to the Expo Center on the man-made island of Odaiba, by Hidetoshi Nagasawa (1995); the poetic Foggy Forest, a work by the artist Fujiko Nakaya in collaboration with Atsushi Kitagawa + ILCD, set within the Showa Memorial Park in Tachikawa-shi, in the city's eastern suburbs (1992); the small Nakano Hill Square by Placemedia (1999); and Shiru-ku Road in Suginami, by Kijō Rokkaku (1991-1993).

Studio On Site has produced a further series of interesting examples; they designed the YKK R&D Center in Ryogoku (1993), the layout of the courtyard facing the Novartis Pharma headquarters in Tsukuba (1993) and, especially, Portside Park in Yokohama (1999), in the new Minato Mirai district. The Tokyo Landscape Architects also worked in the same area, with their Grand Mall Park, created in 1989. It is located in front of Kenzō Tange's Yokohama Museum of Art, which was completed the same year: a large edifice, conceived in an ambiguous Late modern or Postmodern style.

Kiyose Kanayama Green Park, created by Shodo Suzuki in 1986, is an elegant park in Musashino, on the outskirts of the city. The project, poetically dedicated to light and the wind, includes an arid mineral beach that slopes down toward a lake. Akibadai Park (1990) in Hachioji, within the new town of Tama, is instead entirely devoted to games and sport and was designed by the Tokyo Office Heads Co.

Finally, we come to Peter Walker's attractive park behind the IBM Japan headquarters in Makuhari, in the prefecture of Chiba (1991). In spite of

Fujiko Nakaya and Atsushi Kitagawa, Foggy Forest Showa Memorial Park, Tachikawa-shi, 1992

Hidetoshi Nagasawa, Seven Springs Park, Expo Center, Teleport Town, 1995

Shodo Suzuki Kiyose
Kanayama Green Park,
Musashino, Saitama-ken,
1986

Peter Walker, IBM Japan
Technical Center, Makuhari
Building, Chiba-ken, 1991

On site study, Portside
Park, Yokohama, 1999

Gazebo in the Makuhari
Messe gardens, Chiba-ken

Tokyo Landscape
Architects, Grand Mall
Park, Yokohama, 1989

Yoji Sasaki, Sky Forest
Plaza, Shintoshin, Saitama-
ken, 2000

Arc crew, Unerudaiichi
Plaza, Shimbashi,1999

the fact that the American designer is highly active in Japan, and that Walker is considered the true innovator in traditional Japanese landscaping,[4] this is the only work he has realized in the Tokyo metropolitan area.

Theme parks are another story altogether. In addition to the aforementioned Tokyo Disneyland in Urayusu and Sanrio Puroland in Tama, the Tokyo Sea Life Park by Yoshio Taniguchi (1989) is a spectacular aquarium of great architectonic and scenic quality, located along the Edogawa-ku coast, not far from Disneyland. A magnificent glazed cupola constitutes one of its many attractions: it seems to float above a huge, water-filled basin that lies on the roof of the building, most of which is underground, and thus invisible. The waters of the basin visually merge with those of the ocean, so access to the aquarium appears to invite visitors to take a metaphorical dip into the silent depths of the underwater world. Other notable attractions are a large terrace facing over the bay, equipped with enormous, evocative sail-like tensile structures, and a spectacular aqua-theater, where endless numbers of marine creatures can swim freely. Altogether, the complex contains 2000 tons of water.

Wild Blue, Yokohama

Yoshio Taniguchi, Tokyo Sea Life Park, Edogawa-ku, 1989

Yoshio Taniguchi, Tokyo Sea Life Park, Edogawa-ku 1989, Model

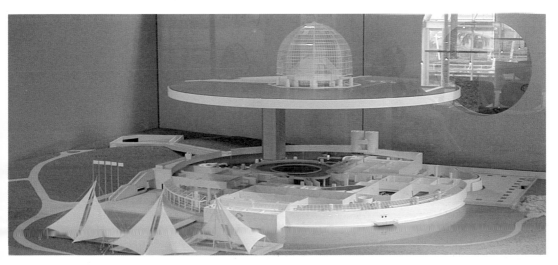

Museums and Cultural Institutions

Museums do not form part of Nipponese tradition. Historically, *Objets d'art* were kept at home as treasures, often in hidden, inaccessible places. Today, however, we must acknowledge that Tokyo has one of the most impressive and comprehensive museum systems on the Asian continent, especially in the arts sector. This may reflect the special attention Japanese culture devotes to the visual arts. Besides, young Japanese artists are the new idols of the international art market. In addition to the highly celebrated Mariko Mori, who is one of the most subtle interpreters of the contemporary Japanese situation, there are names such as Yutaka Sone, Momoyo Torimitsu, Miwa Yanagi and Yoshihiro Suda.

A high concentration of museums is found in one of the city's largest historic parks, Ueno, where Le Corbusier's building also stands. In addition to a recently restored, valuable conservatory from 1890, built in wood by Hanroku Yamaguchi and Masamichi Kuru, several monumental complexes stand out, such as the great Hyokeikan by Tokuma Katayama and Kojiro Takayama (1908), the Tokyo National Museum by Hitoshi (Jin) Watanabe (1937), the Gallery of Eastern Antiquities by Yoshirō Taniguchi (1968), and the Tokyo Metropolitan Art Museum (Tokyoto Bijutsukan) by Kunio Maekawa (1975). Taniguchi's son Yoshio designed the beautiful Hōryūji Gallery (1999), an excellent example of minimalism—all water, reflections and subtle transparency. It houses one of the finest, most prized collections of bronzes, including the first, extremely ancient Japanese im-

Yoshio Taniguchi, Hōryūji Gallery, Ueno Park, Taitō-ku, 1999

Kitutake Architect and Associates, Metropolitan Edo-Tokyo Museum, Yokoami, Sumida-ku, 1992

age of Buddha. The quality of the building was undoubtedly related to the architect's selection for the latest extension to the Museum of Modern Art in New York.

Outside Ueno Park, museums of notable interest include: the National Museum of Japanese History in Satura, in the Chiba prefecture, designed by Yoshinobu Ashihara in 1980; the Museum of Modern Art in Urawa, in the Saitama prefecture (1982), a neorationalist work by Kishō Kurokawa; the Tokyo Metropolitan Art Space in Toshima, again by Yoshinobu Ashihara (1990); the Tepia ("technology" + "utopia") Science Pavilion, devoted to electronic technologies, by Fumihiko Maki (1989), built in the Kita-aoyama area in Minato-ku; the organic Art Museum of Setagaya by Shōzō Uchii (1985); the Mito Art Tower (1990) by Arata Isozaki, distinguished by its soaring tower, a lanmark rising in the Ibaraki prefecture; and the great Museum of Contemporary Art in Kōtō-ku, by Takahiko Yanagisawa and TAK Associated Architects (1994).

The Metropolitan Edo-Tokyo Museum (1992) is entirely dedicated to Tokyo, to its urban history and architecture. A bold, brutal building by Kiyonori Kikutake, it hovers in the air, supported by four huge pillars, harking back to the ancient tradition that kept foodstuffs above the ground to protect them from mice and water. Characterized by a large, double-pitched roof, this colossal museum is accessed from a raised, covered plaza that extends for 18,000 square meters over a large auditorium. Once you have gained access to the building by escalator or elevator, you find yourself in an evocative space, all height, housing a series of interesting documents as well as both scaled and life-size reconstructions of parts of the city and a number of its buildings.

A branch of the above-mentioned museum was opened in 1993, the Edo-Tokyo Open Air Architectural Museum in Koganei City Park. This includes the interesting Temmyō Residence, a great house built in the second half of the 18th century, as well as a reconstruction of Kunio Maekawa's house (1905-86). As mentioned earlier, the architect worked with Le Corbusier in Paris between 1928 and 1930. On his return to Tokyo, he was on Raymond's team from 1930 to 1935, when he opened his own studio. In 1942, despite the war and the restrictions it caused, he built himself a house in Shinagawa. Following the destruction of his Ginza studio in a 1945 bombardment, he used the house as an office, as well. This extremely refined building, entirely built in wood and skillfully balanced between tradition and modernity, was dismantled in 1973, placed into store and then reassembled precisely in the Open Air Museum in 1996, ten years after its creator's death.

Tokyo also has a number of private museums. In Shibuya there is the refined Shoto Museum by Seiichi Shirai (1980), which only houses temporary exhibitions, and Mario Botta's Watari-um (1990), whose interior areas are not very interesting, but whose structure fits well into a corner on a congested block, with a triangular framework rising six stories high. Another interesting building is the small Goto Art Museum by David Chipperfield in Shin-Matsudo, in the Chiba prefecture (1990).

An extraordinarily unconventional example that is practically snubbed by international critics is Makoto Sei Watanabe's K Museum. The small, sculpturesque museum rises on the artificial island of Teleport Town. With its heavy, banded structure in reinforced concrete and steel, it seems to hover above a very cleverly devised piece of artificial landscape.

The Mori Art Museum is the newest private museum, created for the real estate magnate Minoru Mori at the top of the recent Roppongi Hills complex tower. It was inaugurated on October 18th 2003 with an exhibition entitled "Happiness," a recognition of the links between art and life, and of how happiness is multifaceted, according to man's various cultures. Artists on show ranged from Constable and Picasso to Yoko Ono. The museum has also been ambitiously proposed to act as a crossroads for new artists, from Japan in particular and Asia in general: hence the "Roppongi Crossing," an exhibition that will be held triennially, as well as a plan to open a branch soon in Shanghai, at the top of one of the highest new buildings in the world.

A great number of other buildings are devoted to culture in general: theaters, art galleries, libraries, the campuses belonging to more than a hundred universities (including the specialization colleges, now leveled to the rank of Daigaku, i.e. University) and more than eighty high schools in the city—a concrete sign of the prestige enjoyed by culture in general, and education in particular.[5]

Arata Isozaki, Mito Art
Tower Complex, Ibaraki
Prefecture, 1986-90, Model

Arata Isozaki, Mito Art
Tower Complex, Ibaraki
Prefecture, 1986-90,
Western side, section of
the fountain and plans

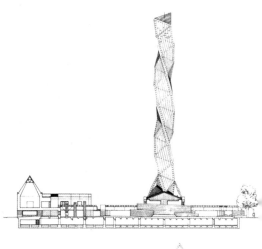

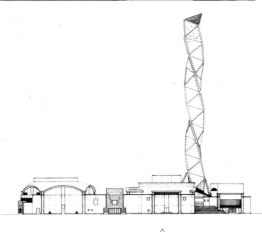

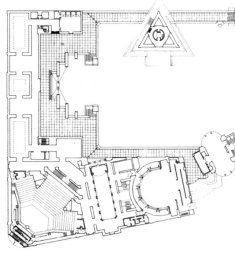

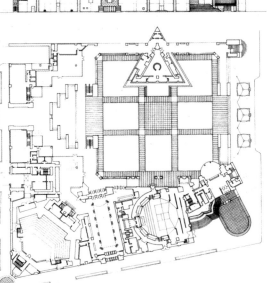

A significant example is the ambiguously Postmodern United Nations University by Kenzō Tange (1992), which, in profile, loosely recalls the façade of Milan's Duomo. It has 14 floors facing onto the elegant Aoyama-dōri in Shibuya and houses an institution which promotes research and training, mostly in the developing countries, under the aegis of the UN.

A small, interesting building in exposed concrete hosts the GA Gallery in Shibuya, created by AMS Architects (Makoto Suzuki and Yukio Futagawa) in 1983 for the Global Architecture publishing house. Natural light illuminates an interior that develops over three levels, housing a gallery and an architectural bookstore.

Other interesting examples are the Keiō University's new library, by Fumihiko Maki (1981) and Shibuya's large multifunctional complex (called Bunkamura) by Jean-Michel Wilmotte and Ishimoto Architects & Engineers (1989), owned by the Tokyu Corporation railway company. In addition to a series of luxury shops and several restaurants, the latter also contains two movie theaters, an art gallery, recording studios, a bookstore and very popular, major concert hall, the Orchard Hall. Additional examples include the Centennial Hall of the Tokyo Institute of Technology in Meguro, by Kazuo Shinohara (1987), characterized by questionable, dissonant, conflictual volumes; the technological Penrose Institute of Contemporary Arts by Nigel Coates/Branson Coates Architects (1993); the Aoyama Technical College by Makoto Sei Watanabe in Shibuya, an unconventional, deconstructed zoomorphic object (1990); the Tokyo Metropolitan Art Space by Yoshinobu Ashihara; the Sōtetsu Cultural Center by Hiroshi Hara + Atelier Phi in Yokohama (1990); the New National Theatre by Takahiko Yanagisawa/TAK Associated Architects and Harald Deilmann (1997); and the Shōnandai Culture Centre by Itsuko Hasegawa (1990). The latter is a complex resulting from a 1986 competition, aimed (doubtfully) at achieving an artificial allegorical landscape. Most of the structure was built underground, and, among other things, it contains a theater and a planetarium; but, with its welcoming open courtyard, the outside area of the complex is better known to visitors.

Mario Bellini's Tokyo Design Center in Shinagawa was built in 1992; it features exhibition areas, a specialized bookstore, a series of furniture showrooms and an Italian restaurant; a monumental bronze horse by Mimmo Paladino dominates the garden at the back.

And here we come to a recent, highly successful children's library by Tadao Ando at the edge of Ueno Park (2000-2002). This newcomer has slipped boldly yet with refined lightness into the dull, preexistent Beaux Arts building; it has improved its external image and brought the interior in line with contemporary needs and taste.

AMS Architects (Makoto
Suzuki and Yukio Futagawa)
GA Gallery, Sendagaya,
Shibuya-ku,1983

Nikken Sekkei, National
Museum of Emerging
Science and Innovation,
Aomi, Kōtō-ku, 2002

Nikken Sekkei, National
Museum of Emerging
Science and Innovation,
Aomi, Kōtō-ku, 2002, plans

Following pages:
Teleport Town

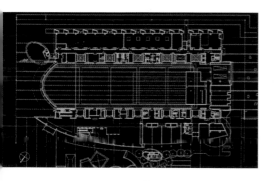
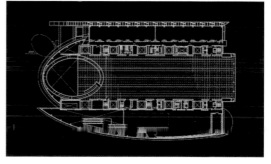

Itsuko Hasegwa, Shōnandai
Culture Center, Fujisawa,
Kanagawa-ken, 1990

Mario Botta, Watari-um
Contemporary Art Gallery,
Jingumae, Shibuya-ku,
1990

青山製図専門学校

Makoto Sei Watanabe,
Aoyama Technical College,
Uguisudanicho, Shibuya-ku,
1990

Mariio Bellini, Tokyo Design
Center, Gotanda,
Shinagawa-ku, 1992

Tadao Ando, International
Children's Library, Ueno
park, Taitō-ku 2000-02,
Addition

Tadao Ando, International
Children's Library, Ueno
park, Taitō-ku 2000-02,
Addition

Kazuo Shinohara,
Centenary Hall, Tokyo
Institute of Technology,
Ōkayama, Meguro-ku,1987

The Towers

Tokyo is now a city of towers, as far as this is possible for such a highly seismic area. But, unlike American downtowns, high-rise buildings have only appeared recently, after World War II (in reality, not before the 1960s). Skyscrapers rise in fragmentary, inconsistent bouts, and do not seem to follow any clear logic, as they are alternated with small and very small buildings. On one hand, this confirms the effective multicentric nature of Tokyo's urban structure, and on the other, a natural coexistence of the old and new, the large and small; but it is also a result of the speed with which the city is growing and developing, as though it had no time for consolidation. Generally speaking, high-rise buildings mostly appear on the most important streets and in the areas near the main subway stations. Immediately behind their vast wings, however, you often find yourself among the small and very small dimensions of Japanese residential tradition. You would be mistaken if you expected to find the historic quality of North American towers in Tokyo: most examples are derivative, often smaller than their precursors and less valuable from an architectural viewpoint. Nevertheless, interesting examples do exist.

What is most important, however, is that as a whole, Tokyo is strongly linked with a high-rise vision. Considering the absence of an urban grid and the uneven, hilly terrain, the presence of skyscrapers creates a disorderly, chaotic city image. But we must add that in the areas with the highest concentration of skyscrapers and, perhaps, especially near the bay, this boundless, irregular rise and fall endows the city with an energy and visual power that is unequaled anywhere in the world: a greater energy than São Paulo, Kuala Lumpur, Pudong in Shanghai or Chicago, and, maybe, even than New York.

The 1960s and 1970s saw the first interesting group of towers, not all in line with contemporary taste. One of the very first towers was the relatively small Sony building by Yoshinobu Ashihara, built in 1966 at one of the most central junctions of Chuo-ku, in Ginza. It was planned as an architectural promenade among the company's electronic products. You take the elevator to the top floor, and then it is convenient to visit the floors by descending the staircase: each floor is subdivided into three exhibition areas, staggered by 90 centimeters.

Undoubtedly, two of the most beautiful and experimental towers of this period were designed by Kenzō Tange/URTEC in 1967, the Dentsū Building in Tsukiji and the offices of the Shizuoka Press and Broadcasting Companies in Ginza. The latter occupies a corner lot close to the elevated Shinkansen railroad; it is a large, 57-meter-high cylinder in reinforced concrete which contains a number of facilities, the staircases and elevators, and a series of projecting bodies that are grafted onto it with constructivist brutality. The whole structure is entirely clad in metal, the same metal that was used for the formworks that produced the castings. The use of metal endows the building with a powerful symbolic significance even today, in spite of its relatively small size compared with more recent structures. There are several recent examples that bear witness to this building's paradigmatic influence. The Sofitel Hotel in Taitō, for instance (1994), by the Kikutake Architect and Associates studio, a 26-story tower, whose odd, saw-tooth profile dominates the small lake of Shinobazu, and the Tokyo University campus.

Yoshinobu Ashihara, Sony Building, Ginza, Chuo-ku 1966

Kenzō Tange, Shizuoka Press and Broadcasting Center. Ginza, Chuo-ku 1967

From the same cultural climate, Kishō Kurokawa's Nagakin Capsule
Tower Building from 1972—also in Ginza—is highly experimental, a vital
part of Tokyo's contemporary architectural image. It was completed a dozen
years after the foundation of the Metabolism group and fully exploits
Kurokawa's experience at the 1970 Osaka Expo. Two towers rising 11 and
13 floors, support 140 protruding, prefabricated metal capsules, each containing an office or a small apartment. Each one is 4 meters long by 2.5
meters wide, has only one circular window, and is equipped with a bed,
wardrobes, a built-in bathroom unit, a television, a clock, a fridge and air
conditioning. Optional extras included a stereo, a sink, table-lamps and a
table calculator. The dialectics between the main megastructure and the plug-
in elements works perfectly. Nevertheless, the building remains one of a kind,
and Kurokawa's later experiments took entirely different directions.

In those years, only a few big studios monopolized the market for im-
portant design contracts. One of these was the Yamashita Architects and
Engineers group, responsible, for example, for the 36-story Kasumigaseki
Building of 1968, which soars 147 meters. This was the first real Japanese

Kishō Kurokawa, Nagakin
Capsule Tower Building,
Ginza, Chuo-ku, 1972

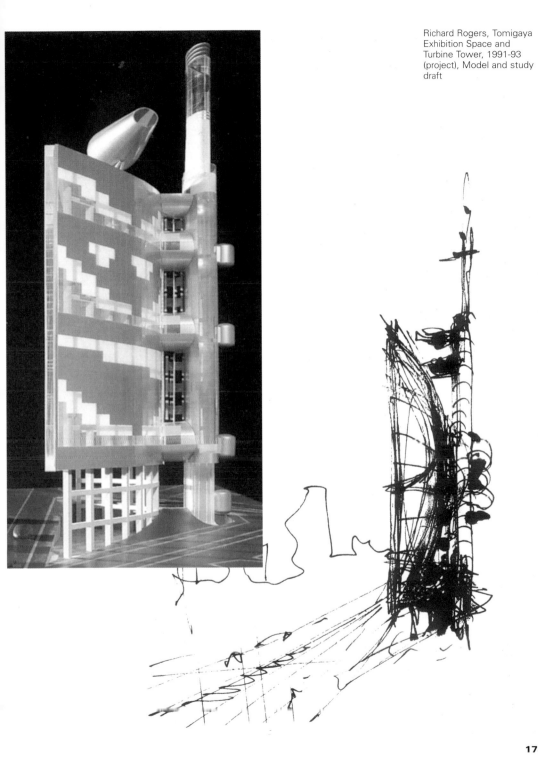

Richard Rogers, Tomigaya
Exhibition Space and
Turbine Tower, 1991-93
(project), Model and study
draft

skyscraper exploiting the increase in height limits, which had been fixed at 31 meters until 1961. It was also the first to use a new American system, FAR (Floor Area Ratio), which provided for possible exceptions in certain isolated cases.

One year before the completion of the building, 107 of the group's planners gathered in the Nikken Sekkei studio, which soon after became the leading Japanese designing company and is now the largest in the world. In 1963, Nikken Sekkei had already built the impressive shopping center in San'ai in Chuo-ku, in Ginza, with its luminous cylinder of only 15 meters in diameter, set on a corner, containing staircases and elevators. It is still one of the district's main landmarks, a prototype of the great number of poster-buildings that were then to populate Tokyo's urban scene during the last decades of the 1900s.

The group's many achievements include the Keiō Plaza Hotel of 1971 in Nishi-Shinjuku, which constitutes Tokyo's first high-rise hotel (47 floors), and was built with a steel framework; the 25-story, asymmetric (until a few years earlier, asymmetry had been banned by aseismatic regulations) Mitsui Building of 1985 in Chiyoda-ku, with a double nucleus for facilities, an empty central space rising to the height of the first four floors, and a light measuring 28 meters; the immensely tall NEC Supertower (1990) in Minato-ku; the Pacifico Yokohama of 1991, a 600-room hotel in a bold sail shape, linked to a large conference center; the headquarters of the Long-Term Credit Bank of Japan, of 1993; the headquarters of the East Japan Railway Company (1997), in Shibuya, yet not far from Shinjuku station—and many others.

Kenzō Tange/URTEC is also responsible for the Akasaka Prince Hotel of 1982-83. An imposing but debatable building, it is distinguished by stepped

Stubbins Associates
Landmark Tower,
Yokohama, 1993

Pacific Yokohama of the
Landmark Tower, 1991

Following pages:
Kenzō Tange, Shinjuku Park
Tower, Nishi-Shinjuku, 1994

volumes, which provides each room with a sizable viewing corner, and an ostentatious hall in white marble, illuminated from above by great skylights.

The Pacific Yokohama is situated in Minato Mirai 21, an extended development on Yokohoma Bay. The colossal complex includes the Landmark Tower, Japan's tallest building, created in 1983 by Hugh Stubbins—who designed New York's Citicorp Center—in collaboration with the Mitsubishi technical office; a multistory shopping mall that you are forced to cross through when leaving the tower's observatory; several hotels; the three scaled, white towers of Queen's Square (1997), also by Nikken Sekkei; and Kenzō Tange's above-mentioned Yokohama Museum of Art.

With its 70 floors, the Landmark Tower soars 296 meters, and is entirely occupied by offices and hotels. The square framework tapers off toward the top and is bordered by four equally sloping corner buttresses. The shape results from a search for greater static efficiency, so as to protect the structure against earthquakes and strong ocean winds. It possibly recalls the curved lines of traditional roofings, but also achieves the effect of an "acceleration" of perspective from below, making the building seem even taller than it is. The observatory affords a view over the entire port and city of Yokohama, and Tokyo's skyline is visible in the distance. On a clear day, you can even make out the conic shape of Fuji; with its 3778 meters of height, the extinct volcano is snow-capped all year round. The ground layout is notable, as well, as it links the tower to the nearby Sakuragichō subway station and to the basin, which contains a spectacular old museum-ship.

The district which is most strongly associated with skyscrapers today is Nishi-Shinjuku, the western side of Shinjuko. Following a systematic policy of decentralization from Marunouchi (the old business and political center lying between Tokyo Station and the Imperial Palace), this became a new high-rise center. This is where the twin towers of the Tokyo City Hall rise, housing the city's metropolitan government, a colossal administrative complex built in 1991 by Kenzō Tange, who turned to Mutō Associates as structural consultants.

The building, firmly anchored to an ambitious urban layout and connected underground to the station of Shinjuku (which is not all that close-by), is mainly made up of a large parallelepiped from which the two actual towers break loose. It was Tange's intention to recall ancient Edo's buildings with its façade, but instead, the front appears to have paid tribute to the international Postmodern trend of the late 1980s. The composition of its masses is similar to that of Nôtre Dame in Paris, but it more closely resembles the austere and sometimes heavy manner with which Perret reconstructed Le Havre. However, the overall image offers great visual power. From Tokyo's highest observatory in one of the two towers, you can enjoy uninterrupted views of the city, spanning 360 degrees. Despite the attention given to details, the considerable care with which it was built and its many symbolic references, the City Hall complex lacks any sense of the human scale and, rather, seems to constitute an architectural representation of the media's power, a factor that is emerging more and more in the city's contemporary spirit.

Cesar Pelli—who designed the huge United States embassy in the Akasaka zone of Minato-ku in 1976 while still working with Gruen Associates in Los Angeles—designed the NTT headquarters (Nippon Telegraph and Telephone Corporation) in Shinjuku, a 1995 tower planned in collaboration with Yamashita Associated Architects. This communications giant, which at that time had just been privatized, turned to a joint Japanese-American group of professionals as a result of the strong pressure exerted by the United States for the liberalization of the building industry, both from a planning and a contracting viewpoint.

The 30-story edifice features a sophisticated curtain wall in glass and aluminum, faced with a silver-gray fluoropolymer finish, linked to a lower section treated with Minnesota stone.

Also at Shinjuko, across the road from the NTT headquarters, rises the Tokyo Opera City Building, a complex including a concert hall, a garden and an art museum, as well as a 54-story office tower.

The complex, designed by the technical office of NTT Power and Building Facilities, the Urban Planning and Design Institute and by TAK Associated Architects (1996), is linked to the adjacent New National Theater by Takahiko Yanagisawa and TAK with Harald Deilmann (1997). The entire complex fits into the planning strategies frequently encountered in Shinjuku, which tend to operate over larger and larger areas of the city, concentrating complementary functions together in huge complexes that are thus turned into powerful attractions for the public.

There are also many hotels in the area (Shinjuku, after all, means "new hotel"). One of the most luxurious is the Park Hyatt, situated inside the Shinjuku Park Tower, also by Tange, a 52-floor skyscraper from 1994, not far from the City Hall complex and made up of three linked towers of decreasing heights.

As a whole, Nishi-Shinjuku offers a sample of downtown American cities, with more or less all of their advantages and disadvantages. Most of the towers are neither attractive nor unattractive, neither low nor particularly high. Nevertheless, they form a powerful, compact whole that marks the skyline forcibly and shows, maybe even flaunts (oddly, in a country so inclined to understatement) Japan's economic power, especially that of the 1980s and 1990s.

The refined Century Tower by Norman Foster (1991) stands out in Bunkyō: a double tower linked by a high atrium diffused with natural lighting. Distinguished by large, exposed metallic beams on the façade, the building is not unlike Foster's earlier, more famous, Hongkong & Shanghai Bank offices in Hong Kong, where Japanese contractors had been involved and where Foster's interest in Japanese building traditions appears in a number of details.

The Ōbayashi Corporation, which was founded in Osaka in 1882, is one of the "Big Five," the five largest Japanese building companies. This company, which, along with other projects, built the historic Tokyo Station, was the client for Foster's work. Through its technical office, it collaborated actively with planning and research into new, suitable approaches. After a series of visits to the Hong Kong skyscraper, the clients

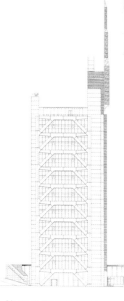

Norman Foster Century Tower, Hongo, Bunkyō-ku, 1991, Eastern perspective

Norman Foster Century Tower, Hongo, Bunkyō-ku, 1991

stipulated an "intelligent" building from the architect. Not only did the response add more sophisticated plant engineering, including floating floors and other features, but it also involved the creation of a highly interactive environment that was pleasantly stimulating for the people working there. The 21 floors of the complex all overlook the sophisticated atrium, which not only is provided with natural lighting from above, but also from a semi-transparent concave plastic surface set at the back. An advanced and totally new system of smoke extraction allowed the plan to go ahead despite strict regulations concerning fire prevention. The building houses an underground art museum, a restaurant, a tea room, a club and more.[6]

Two years later, Foster received a commission for the Ōbunsha Building, another "intelligent" office complex in Shinjuku. This was a double-bodied building with a refined curtain wall and only five floors.

Not far from Tokyo Tower rise the many towers of Roppongi, one of the most lively and dynamic areas of Tokyo. It is dominated by the two towers designed by Cesar Pelli for the aforementioned Mori Building Corporation, one of the leading Japanese property groups. Pelli has worked in Asia extensively. For instance, he designed the twin towers of Petronas in Kuala Lumpur, which are among the highest in the world. Not surprisingly, he is a planner who can guarantee the high level of professionalism that is usually essential to reassure investors involved in property developments of this magnitude.

Still in Roppongi, the Mori Building Corporation has recently built the Roppongi Hills complex (2003). The undertaking, which took 17 years and cost 2.5 billion dollars, includes a huge, 54-story skyscraper by the

Fumihiko Maki, Nippon Convention Center Phase2, North Hall, Makuhari-Messe, 1997

Fumihiko Maki, Nippon
Convention Center Phase1,
Makuhari-Messe, 1989

Following pages:
Fumihiko Maki, Nippon
Convention Center Phase2,
North Hall, Makuhari-
Messe, 1997

American studio Kohn Pederson Fox. The Mori Art Museum and the transparent, sophisticated Asahi TV offices, designed by Fumihiko Maki, are perched at the top. The foot of the complex is dominated by a sculpture of a giant spider by Louise Bourgeois, which was first exhibited at the Tate Modern in London.

A great number of new towers have also risen up around Shinagawa station, at the far south end of the city. Many of them seem to perpetuate the area's original leanings as a hotel area, seeming to hark back to the ancient city port that caused visitors long waits prior to being admitted to the city. The most recent, which are all near the railroad lines, are elegant and transparent, and provide with an ambitious multistory arrangement, pedestrian walkways, parking lots, and shopping arcades.

Another noteworthy group of skyscrapers is to be found in Makuhari, in the Chiba prefecture, in a growing area concentrated around the large fair complex, just beyond Tokyo-to's administrative confines, on the

coastal road leading to Narita airport. Here, among the structures set up for the fair, Fumihiko Maki created two large buildings. The more recent, known as North Hall (1997), features a bold covering structure composed of steel stays.

Yet, most of the newer skyscrapers seem to be concentrated in the dense, high-rise area of Shiodome, squeezed between the rail tracks near Hamamatsu-chō station and the bay. Here, Kevin Roche's elegant tower soars skyward, completely covered in green reflective glass. But the most remarkable building in Shiodome is the Dentsu Tower, an ambiguous, highly refined, lens-shaped building by Jean Nouvel, opened at the end of 2002. Perhaps reminiscent of Gio Ponti's fascinating Milan skyscraper, the tower was completely faced with an iridescent curtain wall in different

KPF, Kohn Pedersen Fox, Roppongi Hills, Minato-ku, 2003. Fumihiko Maki's Asahi TV headquarters are at the top of the tower.

shades of gray that makes its ever-changing presence felt from every point of the bay. It stands in a privileged position overlooking the water, not far from the celebrated, enormous Tsukiji fish market (shortly due to be moved elsewhere), with a series of elegant restaurants on its upper floors that enjoy remarkable views. It was the first tower built by Nouvel and may well be Tokyo's most attractive.

Offices and Multifunctional Complexes

In 1989, Rafael Viñoly, who, like Pelli, is South American (Uruguayan, in this case) and who is also a naturalized United States citizen, took part in the competition for the huge Tokyo International Forum. This was officially approved by the UIA (the Union International des Architectes), and

Kevin Roche, John Dinkeloo & Associates, Shiodome City Center, Higashi-Shimbashi, Minato-ku, 2003

Jean Nouvel, Dentsu Shin
Onsya Office Tower,
Higashi-Shimbashi,
Minato-ku, 2002

Richard Rogers Partnership,
NTV Nittele Tower, Higashi-
Shimbashi, Minato-ku, 2003

Kajima Design, Shiodome
Media Tower, Higashi-
Shimbashi, Minato-ku, 2003

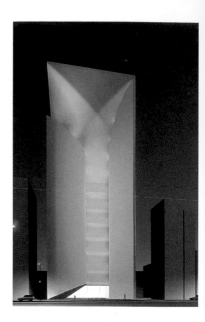

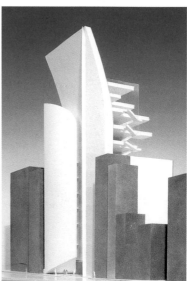

Kajima Design, DaCoMo
Yoyogi Building, Sendagaya,
Shibuya-ku, 2000

Christian de Portzamparc,
Bandai Cultural Center,
1994 (project)

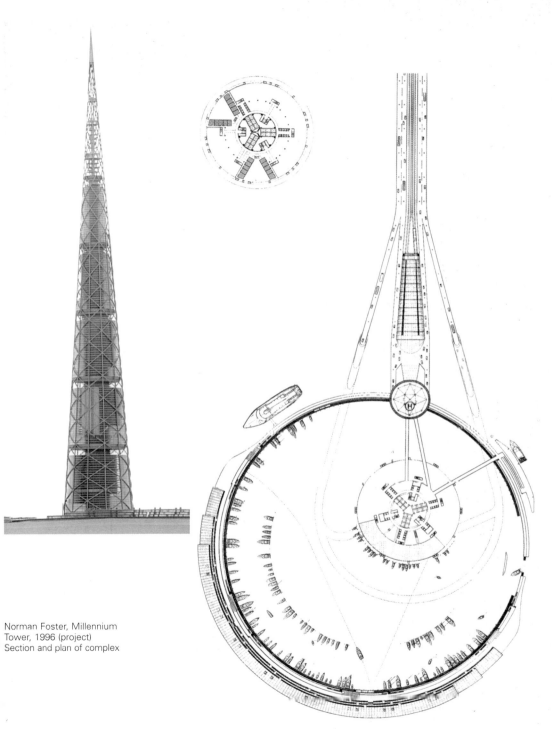

Norman Foster, Millennium
Tower, 1996 (project)
Section and plan of complex

was the first open competition ever announced in Japan. Nearly 400 contenders from 68 countries took part in the competition. The jury included a number of leading names: I.M. Pei, Vittorio Gregotti and Arthur Erickson, as well as the Japanese Kenzō Tange and Fumihiko Maki. Viñoly won, although previously he had only been known for a series of relatively modest projects.

Specifications were for a spectacular complex in the very central, highly congested district of Marunouchi, on an area that is not far from the park surrounding the Imperial Palace and Tokyo Station, which had become vacant following the nonchalant demolition of the City Hall (which, as has been said, was moved to Shinjuku)—a fine example from 1952 produced by Tange himself. Its replacement was to occupy 2.7 hectares, 2 of which could hold buildings, and was to be formed by three massive auditoriums (the largest holding over 5,000 spectators), a large exhibition hall and a considerable number of other facilities, all above a large underground station.

The budget was substantial and grew with time, as the value of the yen steadily appreciated. By the time works were completed in 1996, it had reached approximately one billion dollars. The most remarkable public part of the project is the transparent Glass Hall: an elongated, narrow lens whose planimetry is such that it "leans" on the Japan Railways tracks, with its trains—including the Shinkansen high-speed train—rushing silently by. The geometry of the hall is in line with the trend of the period, and has been propounded and repropounded by various architects in various contexts, so it is more or less justified by its forebears. But here, it undoubtedly appears in its greatest, most spectacular form; 63 meters high by 210 meters long and closed off to the railway, it offers magnificent interior perspectives and extraordinary effects of psy-

Rafael Viñoly, Tokyo International Forum, Marunouchi, Chiyoda-ku, 1996
Zenithal view

Rafael Viñoly, Tokyo International Forum, Marunouchi, Chiyoda-ku, 1996

Rafael Viñoly, Tokyo
International Forum,
Marunouchi, Chiyoda-ku,
1996

Rafael Viñoly, Tokyo
International Forum,
Marunouchi, Chiyoda-ku,
1996

Rafael Viñoly, Tokyo
International Forum,
Marunouchi, Chiyoda-ku,
1996

chological suspension. It is cut through by a series of connecting, diagonal aerial walkways that add great drama to the already impressive space, reminiscent of Piranesi. At the same time, it is completely transparent toward the interior, tree-lined courtyard, a welcoming, well-furnished pedestrian plaza that, except from during lunch hours, is certainly underused. The roofing is a technological, transparent, overturned hull in glass and steel, supported solely by two colossal, sculptural, tapered pillars. The size of the complex gives it great prominence on an urban scale, without its becoming a monument. Swallowed up by the surrounding buildings and not much taller than most of them, in its own way the Tokyo Forum is subtly contextual and mostly displays its undeniable spatial qualities on the inside.

Obviously, the service sector is not only confined to tall buildings. One interesting example comes from Arata Isozaki in 1987, with the Ochanomizu Square Building in Chiyoda-ku. This houses the headquarters of the Shufu-no-tomo publishing house, as well as offices, a concert hall and various other facilities. The image of the new block (which rises on the site of a former building that was in a vague Neoclassical style) closely recalls the successful Tzukuba Centre Building (1983), also built

Arata Isozaki, Ochanomizu
Square Building,
Kandasurugadai
Chiyoda-ku, 1987

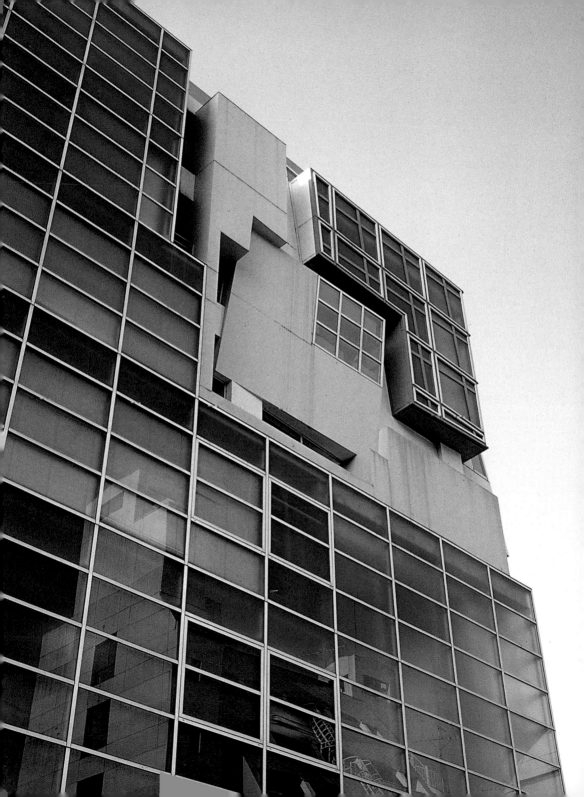

by Isozaki in the center of Tsukuba Science City. The project includes an oval piazza that gained immediate fame, and which is suggestive of Michelangelo's Campidoglio in Rome. As if in confirmation of its creator's fame for "schizophrenic mannerism," as soon as the complex was finished, a series of drawings was rapidly released, portraying it as a disquieting architectural ruin, not unlike what Sir John Soane had done with the 19th century Bank of England project.

Other interesting examples come from two small witnesses of architectural deconstructionism created by Peter Eisenman immediately after the celebrated exhibition, "Deconstructivism" organized by Philip Johnson and Mark Wigley at the Museum of Modern Art in New York. One is the Koizumi Lighting Theater/IZM (1990) in Chiyoda-ku, not far from Akihabara station, in one of the Tokyo areas that is almost entirely dedicated to the sale of electronic goods; the other is the Nunotani Building, in the less easily accessible area of Edogawa-ku (1992). The former is set within a normal Late-Modern building enclosed by a curtain wall of dark glass, and was designed by Kojiro Kitayama, commissioned by an Osaka company specializing in lampshades. Eisenman's contribution is the entrance, a long architectural promenade and a small but spectacular exhibitive setting for the products.

The geometrical plan is strongly subversive and acts as a critical challenge to the solidity of Western architectural tradition. Interesting aesthetic results are achieved through the conflictual use of surfaces and volumes, creative interaction between different spaces, bright colors and a masterful play of natural and artificial lighting effects. It is an intellectual, and in many ways a virtuoso project, a small sample of exceptional bravura, a surprising exploration of the "geometries of instability" that were so fashionable at the time, emotionally absorbing and even today most disquieting.

Eisenman's Nunotani Building was, instead, built in collaboration with the Zenitaka Corporation. It is an office complex with several annexed exhibition galleries. Here, the architect concentrated on the "seismic" instability of architecture, understandably a very seriously approached topic in Japan. Eisenman could not avoid controversy on the way he handled the problem here. He also returned to the theme in subsequent, more demanding projects: the Columbus Convention Center and the Aronoff Center in Cincinnati, both in Ohio. Obviously, the exterior white shell is what actually appears deconstructed here, while, as requested by the clients, the floors have been wisely left horizontal on all levels. Following a change of use designation, the building has recently undergone several radical and inappropriate changes.

From a spatial viewpoint, experiencing similar projects is actually destabilizing, and therefore quite interesting, even though it is not always pleasant from a psychological point of view. It is common knowledge that the great Columbus Convention Center has found itself in difficult situations, precisely because of the strong sense of uncertainty and instability that it communicates to its users. Nevertheless, the role played by Eisenman on the international architectural scene in the 1980s

Peter Eisenman, Nunotani
Corporation Building, Chuo,
Edogawa-ku, 1993
Model

Richard Rogers, Kabuki-chō
Building Offices, Shinjuku-
ku, 1993
Construction detail of the
conservatory support
system

and 1990s was so significant and his influence so widespread that his two
Tokyo examples have gained great importance in defining his experimental architectural journey, one of the 20th century's most fascinating
adventures.

In 1990, the great Australian embassy appeared, designed by Denton
Corker Marshall Pty Ltd, in one of the most attractive lots of Mita's luxurious residential area. The façades, which are mostly clad in aluminum
and steel, make a pleasing contrast with the historic garden the building faces.

The same year The Wall was built, a creative edifice in Nishi-Azabu,
also in Minato-ku, by the British studio Branson Coates Architecture.
Marked by history, it appears like a sort of ruin from Ancient Rome.

One year later, a small multifunctional building was designed by TAO
Architects in Hamamatsuchō. Here, too, the façade is characterized by
aluminum, stretched out in blades to shape a menacingly sharp prow.

Buildings of such an experimental nature are spread everywhere. Another impressive example is constituted by Joule-A, a bold building by
Edward Suzuki, distinguished by a "broken" and "ripped" metal façade.
This has various uses (residences, offices, parking lots and a club-restau-
rant, in addition to a Rolls Royce and Aston Martin car dealer).

In 1992, one of the most productive years, two interesting multifunctional complexes (with residential and shopping areas as well as offices) were built by Riken Yamamoto and Field Shop: the technological,
articulated, multistory XISTUS and G-F Building. These were included
in a group of projects that were part of the ambitious Inter-Junction City

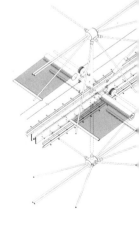

Edward Suzuki, Joule-A
Shopping Center,
Azabujuban, Minato-ku,
1990

Richard Rogers, Kabuki-chō
Building Offices, Shinjuku-
ku, 1993
North view

TAO architects, Gill
Building, Hamamatsuchō,
Minato-ku, 1991

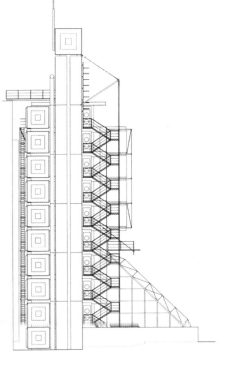

in Yokohama. A year later, ARCUS, by the same planners, joined the series. The building, like those above, includes an interior pedestrian passageway on the second floor, connected to the other semipublic areas by staircases and elevators, namely to a basement plaza and terraces on the higher levels. The usual coexistence of reinforced concrete for the main structures and steel for the secondary ones (overhanging roofs, walkways, balconies, sunshading screens etc.) is accompanied by the use of glass to cover the central walkway.

Yamamoto is a sophisticated planner; his experimentation was mostly directed toward enhancing the interior pedestrian walkways within the various complexes, so as to make them more interesting from an architectural viewpoint. He also replicated the "ground floor" effect higher up. But his main concern was to make it easier to open businesses in protected, welcoming environments. As a whole, the planning of Inter-Junction city was aimed at inaugurating a new way of life that could be copied in adjacent buildings, designed by different architects—which is what actually happened in several successful cases.

Another significant multifunctional complex also appeared in 1992, this time in Nagayama, in the heart of the aforementioned new town of Tama. It is a complex, chaotic composition by Toyo Ito, harmonized only by its exterior aluminum facings. It houses a series of recreational fa-

Kanko Kikaku Sekkeisha,
Le Meridien Grand Pacific
Tokyo, Ariake, Koto-ku,
1998

cilities that are open to the public: health spas, restaurants, banquet halls, a bowling alley, a videogame center and a karaoke bar.

In 1993, a small ten-story building by Richard Rogers (with Architect 5 Partnership) was erected in the chaotic, congested area of Kabuki-chō, in Shinjuku. Entirely glazed and characterized by a semisubterranean atrium that was meant for a restaurant, it now appears as an unfortunate example of High-Tech, and has been somewhat neglected and forgotten.

One of the most spectacular buildings of Teleport Town, the artificial island in the bay, is the Fuji Television headquarters (1996) by Kenzō Tange: huge and open to controversy, it appears like an emblematic representation of the city's media-oriented nature. The complex houses television production and broadcasting companies, and, as often happens in Tokyo, a recreational center open to the public, as well.

Here, Tange chose to use an ambiguous perforated block measuring 210 meters lengthwise and 120 meters in height, the maximum allowed on the island. The structure is actually composed of two towers that rise up from a common uplifted base, linked by walkways that are set at six-story intervals.

The colossal foundation plinth comprises television studios, a theater and a multistory parking area; a terraced garden was created on the sev-

enth floor. This is reached by outside staircases and escalators; access to the elevators can only be gained here. The whole is uniformly faced in aluminum and glass. A large sphere, 32 meters in diameter, is faced in titanium, and is precariously fitted into the top of the building: it houses an observatory and a restaurant. Half-way between a science fiction film and one of Piranesi's prisons, the building is much loved by tourists due to its glorious views toward the city, the bay and Rainbow Bridge; it is also a fascinating example of "visionary rationalism," in Franco Purini's convincing interpretation of the term.

Another impressive complex on the island is the so-called "Tokyo Big Sight," or International Exhibition Center, an enormous structure realized in 1995 by Axs Satow Inc.: a center featuring 80,000 square meters of fair, exhibition and conference space, including auditoriums (the largest holding 1,000 seats), situated at the extreme southeastern corner of Teleport Town's main pedestrian area, adjacent to the Yurikanome Line monorail station. The main body, made up of four inverted pyramids resting on a square base and opening out toward the sky, is ambiguously reminiscent of an oil rig. Not far away lies Tokyo Fashion Town, a center that has set itself the ambitious target of gathering all fashion-related creative activities in one spot. This linear, technological complex was built in 1996 by Kenzō Tange, Nihon Sekkei and Yamashita Sekkei. A number of busy restaurants are located in its entrance hall and on the terraces overlooking the bay.

Sato Sogo Keikaku, Tokyo Big Sight Exhibition Center, Ariake, Kōtō-ku, 1995

Foreign Office Architects,
Port Terminal, Yokohama,
2002
Interior

Foreign Office Architects,
Port Terminal, Yokohama,
2002

Philippe Starck and
M. Nosawa, Unhex Nani-
Nani Building, Shirokanedai,
Minato-ku, 1989
Model

Philippe Starck and
M. Nosawa, Unhex Nani-
Nani Building, Shirokanedai,
Minato-ku, 1989

Philippe Starck and
M. Nosawa, Asahi "Super
Dry Hall," Azumabashi,
Sumida-ku, 1989

Like Eisenman, Philippe Starck also created two emblematic buildings: the small Unhex Nani-Nani, a zoomorphic monster completely covered in green metal scales, and the even showier Asahi Biru Honsha (1989), better known as the "Super Dry Hall," built for Asahi, a large Japanese brewery. The latter, located in the Asakusa quarter—the ancient temple district—includes an elegant restaurant and is surmounted by an enormous, ambiguous golden horn, "la Flamme d'Or" or, as the signs at the entrance say, a great drop of beer.

Another interesting work is Toyo Ito's Community Complex in Yokohama (1996-97), which includes a day-care center for the elderly, a community center and a gym. A refined, composed and transparent building, it has a sober chromatic range and features an interplay of natural and artificial light in its interior areas.

Again, one of the latest, most interesting works is to be found in Yokohama: the Port Terminal (2002), resulting from an international competition won by Foreign Office Architects. It features some of the best architecture of the digital age. Farshid Moussawi and Alejandro Zaera-Polo, who were only in their thirties when entries closed for the competition (1994)—which saw extensive participation from every part of the world—created and realized a changeable, dynamic "liquid" architecture made up of flows and shifts. Horizontal floors bend and meet one another with no separating walls; glass sheets close the remaining openings. The structure is entirely dressed in steel; the exterior wooden facings, which are gently shaped on "geological," double-curved surfaces, are like sailboat decks; the creative, precarious handrails are in steel. The infrastructure accommodates cruise liners and boats offering tourist trips around the bay, but it also constitutes Yokohama's most attractive urban "piazza," a place where you can enjoy the panorama of an extraordinary skyline: "a hybrid between ship-building and origami" and especially, "a hybrid of landscape and building."[7]

Stadium spotlight,
Yokohama

Sport

Some of the best sporting facilities of the 1980s, both of which pay tribute to Kenzō Tange's seminal work for the 1964 Olympic Games, are two works by Fumihiko Maki: the Municipal Gymnasium in Fujisawa (1984), with complex, fleeting geometries, located on the edge of the city in the prefecture of Kanagawa; and the even more surprising sports hall in Shibuya (1988-90), set within a broad complex in which various elements (swimming pools, gyms, tennis courts) are all marked out by different roofings (like a shell, a ziggurat, or waves). The most notable, original feature here is undoubtedly a bold, silvery covering supported by a large pair of metallic arches anchored within reinforced concrete extensions. The Tokyo Dome, which is adjacent to a famous park belonging to the Edo period, was created by Nikken Sekkei jointly with the Takenaka Corporation in 1988. This baseball stadium for 50,000 spectators—also used for other sporting events, fairs and concerts—is covered by an airtight membrane coated in fiberglass, whose pressure is constantly kept under control. The Tokyo Budōkan in Adachi-ku, an extensive complex for mar-

Kajima Design, Lala Port
"Swas" Ski Dome,
Funabashi, Chiba-ken
Prefecture, 1993

Fumihiko Maki, Tokyo
Metropolitan Gymnasium,
Sendagaya, Shibuya-ku,
1990

tial arts, is a debatable work, built in 1989 by Kijō Rokkaku along with Hanawa Structural Engineers. Finally, we come to a great oddity: the Ski Dome by Kajima Design (1993) in Funabashi, in the Chiba prefecture, along the coastal road connecting Tokyo to Narita airport. This is a 100-meter-high aseismatic steel structure supporting a sloping sheet of concrete measuring 500 meters lengthwise. A ski slope with a 7% to 20% gradient was created over this, and is reached by a chairlift. Annexed to the slope are a swimming pool, a sauna, restaurants and various shopping areas. The interior temperature is maintained at 2°-6° C.

Shopping

The cult of shopping is one of the main driving forces behind a consumer society. If this is truer in Japan than anywhere else, it is mainly due to the country's considerable wealth. As we have seen, from the 1960s to the early 1990s, the economy was marked by unprecedented growth. From the poverty it experienced after the war, Japan became one of the wealthiest countries in the world. The luxury goods industry took advantage of a large number of potential purchasers, mostly consisting of high-income young people with a great propensity to spend, and of the growing success of exported Japanese-made and designed products. This is true right across the country, but especially in Tokyo, where average earnings are significantly higher than anywhere else.[8] As regards fashion in particular, production is concentrated in Sumida and wholesale sales in Nihonbashi, while the main centers for design, exhibition and retail sales are in Ginza, Harajuku and Aoyama.

The 1990s crisis, which was predominantly financial, did not really affect citizens' spending habits. It has been calculated that the Japanese could go on supporting their high standard of living for another 20 years, even without an economic upturn. The country has considerable reserves and continues to display exceptional production capacity. In short, in Tokyo people spend money on all sorts of things and buy all sorts of things, (almost) as though nothing had happened. It is a population of fashion victims for whom shopping is absolutely imperative; on the shopping altar, everything is unhesitatingly sacrificed. Here, more than anywhere else, shopping assumes the dimensions of a mass sociological phenomenon, so the architectural structures devoted to the sale of luxury goods form an important part of the urban image. We are referring to interiors, but also to entire buildings that follow precise rules in which the plan is often transformed into concept design, an illustration of a broader philosophy of life and behavior.

The "depato"—a Japanese corruption of "department stores"—and shopping malls contain a series of extremely interesting examples: Takashimaya, Matsuya, Shirokiya, Matsuzakaya and so on. Among them, some illustrious historical examples stand out, such as the Mitsukoshi headquarters in the central area of Nihonbashi, a large Neo-Renaissance building built in 1927 by Tamisuke Yokokawa. The name Mitsukoshi was registered in 1928 but the company has been active since ancient times; in fact, it goes back to the Edo period when Mitsui Takatoshi (1622-94)

Aldo Rossi, Showroom
Ambiente, Minami Aoyama,
Minato-ku 1991

opened his first emporium in the city—bearing witness to the city's early mercantile vocation.

The need to attract clients has led to a risky, debatable use of design
devices. A recent borderline case where the scenography has pursued a
Baroque taste is to be found in the Venus Fort, on the man-made island
of Teleport Town. The complex, similar to the Forum Shops in Las Vegas, reproduces a whole sequence of piazzas, streets, openings, monu-
ments, fountains etc. in "Italian style" and with improbable Italian place
names, covered by an artificial sky, which varies according to the changes
in the natural sky outside, without, obviously, running any risk from at-
mospheric agents.

Today, Tokyo is also one of the world capitals of the streetwear that
has so influenced traditional haute couture, overturning concepts of taste
in just a few decades. The spaces devoted to retail sales, mostly aimed
at the young and very young, follow precise rules; novelty constitutes an
absolute value, even if not everything that is new automatically becomes
valuable. Selling products requires an appropriate, innovative image. Spe-

211

Fumihiko Maki, Spiral
Building/Wacoal Art Center,
Minami Aoyama, Minato-
ku, 1985

Tadao Ando, Shopping
Center Collezione, Minami
Aoyama, Minato-ku, 1989

Tadao Ando, Shopping
Center Collezione, Minami
Aoyama, Minato-ku, 1989

H. Wakabayashi, Humax Pavillion Department Store, Udagawacho, Shibuya-ku, 1992

Jun Aoki, Louis Vuitton Omotesando Shop, Jingumae, Shibuya-ku, 2002

Following pages: Renzo Piano, Hermes Building, Ginza, Chuo-ku, 2002

cialized interior designers and architects have to mediate constantly between the need to feed the market with new ideas and that of answering the unpredictable demands and expectations of consumers. At the first sign of a drop in sales, there is a change in direction, and, especially, renovation of the sales areas.

Due to the city's size, the same type of competitiveness that usually occurs between different cities takes place within Tokyo itself. For some time, the commercial supremacy of Ginza (the "place of silver," where jewelers used to be concentrated) has risked being compromised by the aggressive commercial policy of other parts of Tokyo. For years, Shinjuku, Shibuya and especially the area of Minami Aoyama have attracted an endless series of extraordinary and highly experimental shopping areas.

Many examples are also dedicated to design: from Ambiente International (1981), a small, debatable building by Aldo Rossi (which includes the signature of Morris Adjimi, then the head of Rossi's New York studio) in Minami Aoyama, to the recent, transparent, minimalist showroom devoted to Kazujo Sejima's furnishings in a small pedestrian area much frequented and loved by young people, between the Shibuya and Harajuku stations. There are also a number of multifunctional complexes in which, as we have already seen, commerical activities mix with cultural

Renzo Piano, Hermes
Building, Ginza, Chuo-ku,
2002

Future Systems with
R. Kawakubo and
T. Kawasaki, Comme des
Garçons, Minami Aoyama,
Minato-ku, 1999

and recreational areas. Take, for example, two high-quality examples also to be found in Minami Aoyama: Fumihiko Maki's Spiral Building, built in 1985, an ambiguous, slightly deconstructed building characterized by a great interior spiral staircase; and the equally famous Collezione by Tadao Ando (1989). This is not in such a prime position but has the usual exposed concrete and an elaborate spatial geometry that plays on the conflictual insertion of a cylindrical volume into a main parallelepiped and two smaller bodies.

But the highest degree of creativity is to be found in one-brand stores: these boutiques often occupy entire buildings created ad hoc. In Tokyo, "to make an architectural fashion statement here, it is no longer enough to create a shop interior, no matter how exquisite. To stand out in this shifting seascape of an environment, you need to build something on the scale of a super-tanker, if you are really going to register."[9]

A first example of the simplified use made of the hackneyed Postmodern architectural vocabulary comes from the showroom in Harajuku created by Ricardo Bofill and his Taller de Arquitectura, in collaboration with Kajima Design, for United Arrows (1992). The glazed façade is marked by superimposed pairs of basic columns on three levels, made to look like stone.

Examples coming from the aggressive commercial policies of Issey Miyake and Comme des Garçons are more interesting. The most memorable are the Pleats Please boutiques in Marunouchi (1999) and Aoyama (2000), and Me Issey Miyake in Shibuya (2001), all designed by Curiosity, a studio formed by Nicolas Gwenael and Reiko Miyamoto. Comme des Garçons has also made use of various designers, but always in collaboration with the celebrated stylist Rei Kawakubo. The most successful boutique is Future Systems in Minami Aoyama, from a collaboration with Takao Kawasaki, distinguished by the "blue wave" of its gigantic window.

Paul Smith, instead, turned to Sophie Hicks, working with the artist Richard Wood in Shibuya and with the photographer Marc Quinn in Daikanyama, while Yohji Yamamoto chose Yasuo Kondo for his Ginza boutique, dominated by a display of long, sinuous steel tapes.

Jun Aoki, who had already designed the Nagoya outlet in 1999, created the Louis Vuitton building in 2002, a spectacular, sophisticated multistory edifice enclosed by superimposed translucent and mirrored panels that create a moiré effect, and surfaces of mirror-finished and golden steel. On the top floor a spacious, double-height terrace opens up, facing onto Omotesando, an elegant tree-lined avenue much frequented by the capital's fashion victims, right in front of the famous Dojunkai residences built after the 1923 earthquake. For the interior, an original 1990s concept by Peter Marino was simply updated. The day it was inaugurated, an orderly queue of 1,400 people waited at length for their turn to cross the threshold. Japan on its own accounts for one third of the brand's turnover, and 2002 saw a 16% increase.

One of the most celebrated architects who have worked in this sector is Renzo Piano, with Hermès, sited on one of the most central, crowded corners of Ginza. The building, practically a 15-story *maison de verre* on a long, narrow framework, is entirely faced with specially forged glass bricks featuring mobile, vibratile surfaces bordered with mirrored silvering. Rena Dumas fitted the sales floors out soberly; Hilton McConnico set up an elegant museum on the fifth floor, devoted to the Hermès iconographic tradition; the 13th and 14th floors contain a double-height art gallery, and the top story opens up onto a sophisticated roof garden in Japanese taste.

Also in Omotesando, and in association with the Takenaka Corporation, in 2003 Jacques Herzog & Pierre de Meuron designed a transgressive, transparent sales point for Prada; a six-story blue-green crystal enclosed by a continuous, diagonal, bee-hive steel mesh. The work leaves a large outside area free to the public—a generous gesture, given the very high land values in the area. Within the building, the cold, refined spaces seem to be inspired by the all-Japanese theme of emptiness. But the surfaces change continuously, and from jellylike turn to damp, mossy, hairy or viscous; the furnishings are covered in materials ranging from pony skin to silicone to optic fibers: it is a triumph of physicality and tactility. The changing rooms are transparent but can be made opaque on request. The cost is estimated at 80 million dollars.

Finally, the most recent undertakings (2003-04) in the same area feature the cold, transparent Christian Dior buildings, created by Kazuyo Sejima and Ryue Nishizawa, as well as Tod's, by Toyo Ito.

J. Herzog and
P. de Meuron, Prada Store,
Minami Aoyama, Minato-ku,
2003
Model

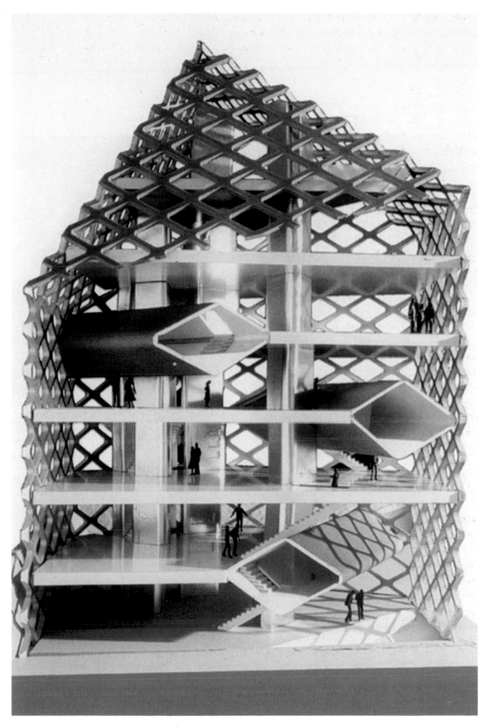

[1] V. Gregotti, "Una modernità dis-orientata," in *Casabella*, no. 608-609, 1994.
[2] A. Berque, "La città Giapponese, Uso di un'immagine," in *Casabella*, no. 608-609, 1994.
[3] Cf. *Toyo Ito*, edited by S. Roulet, S. Soulis. Paris: Moniteur, 1991. Quoted in N. Tajima, *Tokyo*. Köln, Könemann, 1996, p. 84.
[4] Cf. A. Villari, *L'architettura del paesaggio in Giappone*. Rome: Gangemi, 2002.
[5] Data from 1987. Cf. F. Mariani, *Ore Giapponesi*. Milan: Corbaccio, 2000, p.78 Or. Ed. 1956.
[6] Cf. C. Davies, I. Lambot, *Century Tower. Foster Associates build in Japan*, Hong Kong: Watermark Publications, 1992.
[7] R. Moore, "Punto di partenza," in *Domus*, no. 851, September 2002.
[8] Cf. S. Sassen, *The Global City, New York, London, Tokyo*, Princeton: Princeton University Press, 1991 p. 238.
[9] D. Sudjic, "Cultura e mercato," in *Domus*, no. 861, July-August 2003.

Marni Ometesando Shop, Minami Aoyama, Minato-ku, 1999-2000

Research Institute of Architecture, Q Front Stores, Udagawacho, Shibuya-ku, 1999

7. The Liquid Room

We could continue our "excursus" on the city's architecture at length, talking of ever newer and more surprising buildings. But this is not the point. Tokyo, today more than ever, is an extraordinary—possibly the most extraordinary—showcase of contemporary architecture: a capital of architecture. But it is also true that, despite everything, this is totally subordinated to the exceptional, overwhelming power of the city. Architecture must be searched out from an infinite sea of buildings and it is difficult, if not impossible, for architectural quality to emerge and be noticed. This holds for the international stars too, even when the budgets are so huge as to be almost unthinkable by European standards.

The gap between architecture and the city or, more generally, between architecture and urban culture, was cogently expressed by Vittorio Gregotti when, in his 1994 editorial significantly entitled *A Dis-orientated Modernity* he wrote: "The Japanese architecture featured in specialized journals is ample in quantity and often of morphological and technical quality. Nevertheless any attempt to deduce a portrait of the country from such coverage is a nearly impossible task, even when the clues provided are examples of the finest work being done there. The minimalist religiosity of Tadao Ando, the eclectic exoticism of Arata Isozaki, the interpretative precision of Fumihiko Maki, the technical and formal lightness of Yamamoto, the poetic calm of Shinohara, are signals, in which the sublimation of contemporary Japan achieves a level of lofty, refined detachment. But behind the formal quality of these reports, it is also easy to glimpse a nation which, during the last thirty years has assumed a new, tumultuous, often violent identity, in which the new generations appear driven by a restless desire to break the limitations of the work ethic and tradition, in a form of extreme hybridization, at odds with the nation's pride in its productivity."[1]

Hence Tokyo emerges as a city where, on closer inspection, the strongest, most persistent impression comes not from its architecture (as it has, for example, in Berlin over the last decades) but more from its chaotic mass of buildings, from the invasive infrastructure already discussed and, even more, from the gigantic electronic hyper-surfaces in Shibuya, Shinjuku and Ginza (but not from the buildings that simply constitute their physical support). Entire, endless quarters bring something of New York's Times Square or London's Piccadilly Circus to the urban scale, operating day and night, night especially, as prodigious, hypnotic radiators of images in movement and sound. The spectacle is dazzling and hallucinogenic, one in which Tokyo is revealed as a place of "samsara," in Sanskrit the "running around," or of "ukiyo-e," the ambiguous, fleeting, "floating world."

Shibuya-ku

223

This dynamic virtual dimension adds to and outweighs the already very powerful one of highly ordered chaos that comes from escalators and travelators (on which the few people standing still have to remain strictly on the left, just like cars, to let those in a hurry pass on the right); from the multiplicity of levels; from the continual flows of very fast trains and of cars which, with the obsession for safety shared by all advanced countries, do not exceed 40 kilometers per hour in the city (more than from private vehicles, which can be registered only by those who have a parking space, this comes mostly from taxis, with their immaculate little linings and doors that, for hygiene, open and close automatically so they don't have to be touched by human hand, driven by highly trustworthy drivers in white gloves); and from the endless masses of pedestrians who move quickly at rhythms imposed by traffic lights, lonely and solipsistically concentrated on the color displays of their new generation mobile phones. "You feel uneasy, dazed, inebriated, depending on the moment and spiritual disposition, by the Ganges-like, Amazon-like rivers of human beings—especially at rush hours."[2] It is a multi-ethnic, talented, creative crowd, made up of tribes of anarchic-looking youngsters, often aggressive and rude, inspired by "manga" (comics), the films of Kitano Takeshi, the music of Sakamoto Ryūichi, or the characters in the stories of Banana Yoshimoto and Haruki Murakami, yet who never seem to lose sight of "style" and ordered, civilized, disciplined behavior.

We are probably facing an entirely new urban phenomenon; maybe the whole architectural and urban situation is going through a process of mutation. The roots of the phenomenon were growing throughout the entire second half of the last century. Isozaki recalls that, "during the

Teleport Town of the Yurikanome Line

war, in many Japanese cities all form was lost, then they were rapidly filled by buildings that from the start looked like ruins, lacking any visual order: steel and reinforced concrete mixed with advertising sheets, neon lights and telephone poles. The cities lost their massive solidity behind accumulations of oscillating, light, superficial elements. They began to transmit their meaning more by semiotic codes than real, solid forms. The city is in a state of fluidity. Invisible, it is virtually simulated by the codes that fill it."[3]

Tokyo, hypermodern megalopolis—of an *ante litteram* modernity, an abyssal, vertiginous modernity that seems to have existed for ever and which, as Barthes observes, "constitutes Japan's uniqueness"[4]—seems today to tend ever more towards the liquid state.

This is obviously a metaphor, but only to an extent, when you think how the "stable," "solid" and "real" characteristics of the city are systematically and progressively giving way to "dynamic," "fluid" and "virtual" characteristics.

The Liquid Room is a large discotheque on the 7th floor of a building by Kabuki-chō in Shinjuku (in the 1990s Massive Attack, a now internationally renowned group, played there). Rivers of hallucinogenic images are projected into a dark space, dematerializing the consistency of the surfaces and transforming them into hyper-surfaces. The volume of the sound and the thousands of people in movement complete the effect. The physical space appears as if transforming into a liquid state.

Not much more, not much less than what occurs in discotheques all over the world. Perhaps this discotheque doesn't exist any more, or perhaps it has changed its name; the name, in any event, is not particularly original. But what is more interesting here is that the concept of

Shibuya-ku

a liquid room, of liquid space, seems to represent the contemporary situation in Tokyo better than anything else. This is the thesis of Zygmunt Bauman's essay entitled "Liquid Modernity,"[5] although its frame of reference is more general, not just urban Japan.

Without presuming to reiterate the arguments expressed in detail by Bauman, which are in any event more sociological in nature, let us try to look at the question from the point of view of architectural creativity. What does "liquid modernity" mean for architecture? Does it mean a metaphorical "liquefaction" of the planning principles underlying modernity, a "liquefaction" of planning in general, or a real, actual "liquefaction" of architectural space? Is it in short possible to talk of a liquid room, of a liquid architectural space, or is this a contradiction in terms? Then, borrowing the rankings introduced by Rem Koolhaas, can the notion of "liquidity" be extended from the average architectural scale-M, to the large or extra-large scale-L or XL (urban or territorial), or the small scale-S (interior design, for example)? And are we sure that we are looking at a metaphorical "liquefaction"—of modernity, of architecture, of its representation or something else—and not instead at a less desirable (to architects at least), progressive, effective "liquidation"? And finally, in regard to this latter, apparently negative hypothesis, could it be that, this is basically a scenario involving less concern than we might think? The architecture and the city, the quality of architectural and contemporary urban space in general and in Tokyo in particular—are these so important to man's life? Does not the radical revi-

Shinjuku-ku

sion that the concept of space has undergone perhaps make more acceptable the fact that its permanence in time is not essential?

A body in the liquid state is, as is well known, characterized by fluidity. This, unlike the solid state, implies the absence of actual shape. Hence space does not remain fixed in time; architecture has, more or less always done the opposite.

A century and a half ago, Karl Marx and Friedrich Engels spoke of "melting solid bodies," a metaphorical condition necessary for the revolution, but also an unreservedly temporary condition; in reality they were hoping for the more or less speedy formation of "new and better solid bodies."

We all know that, probably, "the epoch of systematic revolutions has passed because there no longer exist strongholds of power to expunge, and also because it is extremely difficult, not to say impossible, to imagine what the victors could do, once having penetrated them, to overturn the situation and bring an end to the poverty that led to their rise. Why should we then be surprised by the obvious absence of aspiring revolutionaries, of the people who articulate their desire to end their own sufferings in a plan destined to change the order of society?"[6] But we also know that what is perhaps true in a socio-political sphere, may not be so in the much more fluid sphere of human creativity. We know, for example, that the digital revolution in architectural planning in recent years, a leading element in the debate between real and virtual, has actually been more real than virtual, just as, in other fields, the push to-

wards technological innovation, for instance, or the mobility of capital, social reorganization and cultural transformations, have all been real. We also know how difficult it is to survive a process of liquefaction without this turning into an irreversible liquidation. These are risks that did not escape the notice of Jurgen Habermas when, during exchanges over the success of Deconstructionism during a philosophical debate in the 1980s, he declared: "when the containers of an autonomously developed cultural sphere are shattered, the contents get dispersed. Nothing remains from a desublimated meaning or a destructured form; an emancipatory effect does not follow."[7] Is therefore "liberation"—from formal constrictions, from the fixedness of architectural and urban space—a blessing or a curse? Bauman, echoing the words of Habermas, warned: "What has been shattered can not be stuck back together again. Abandon all hope of totality, future or past, all ye who enter the world of fluid modernity."[8]

As we have said repeatedly, Tokyo's contemporary urban space also tends to the labyrinthine. This is a potent metaphor of our way of thinking about or understanding the future, an image of the human condition that signifies, "the obscure place in which the network of streets might not obey any rules. In the labyrinth it is chance and surprise that reign supreme, witnessing the defeat of pure Reason."[9]

So living becomes "the art of living in the labyrinth." The metropolitan area of Tokyo is today ever more a non-place, hailing less from

Shinjuku building

228

architecture and the traditional definition of spaces than from the ubiquitous, labyrinthine presence of telecommunications networks, intelligent buildings and machines, plant for the accumulation and diffusion of energy and water, waste removal and recycling, and diverse, interconnected transport systems.

As has been widely pointed out, the telematic digital systems bear the same relationship to the contemporary 21st-century city as the ancient water courses, caravan routes, railways and motorway systems did to the old city, from antiquity up until the 20th century. The metaphor of liquidity, in contrast to the solidity inherent in all architecture, also goes to explain the "light" physical invasiveness of the various forms of digital infrastructure. Unlike traditional elements of infrastructure, hydraulics, electricity, railways, roads, motorways, airports etc., the telecommunications sphere takes up less physical space and, in many ways, goes relatively unnoticed: invisible, silent, non-polluting and so on. In this sense it pervades a contemporary city in the same way as a historical one; it works in an ancient European village of mediaeval origin as in an Asian megalopolis. And the process of transforming historical cities into digital cities goes just as unnoticed, endorsing the intuition of many that this tends to lead architecture and its quality towards oblivion.

Tokyo's inhabitants today belong concurrently to different social spheres, the concepts that in 1887 Ferdinand Tönnies had differentiated as Gemeinshaft and Gesellshaft. So you can live within a small com-

munity in a real sense and yet participate in a more extensive, international (or even planetary) community that is virtual or, vice versa, emigrate to a distant city while remaining in contact with a small original nucleus of family or friends[10]. The notion of the community of individuals, the *civitas* referred to in the first chapter of this work, comes out of it all profoundly modified; today it is an interactive hybrid suspended between reality and virtuality. The difference between near and far has patently been annulled in favor of that sort of extra-territorialism that is precisely what the net is.

Therefore the city is ever more a place of exchange and interaction between virtual and real, between the digital sphere and urban reality and physical architecture. This happens at various levels, from the gigantic screens of the Japanese capital to the virtual dining room proposed some years ago by IBM, a restaurant where you could eat and converse with a virtual fellow-diner on the other side of a screen dividing the table in two—a person physically distant but present and able to talk to you while you were eating.

Buildings tend to appear as a diverse array of hyper-surfaces. These have meaningful precedents in the inscriptions and figurations superimposed on the great buildings of classical antiquity, on gothic cathedrals stained glass, on the neon lights of Las Vegas during the second half of the 20th century. Buildings accommodate and support various forms of virtuality, allowing them to provide, for instance, different information in different idioms: toponomastic to help orientate passers by, historical-critical for tourists, technical for maintenance workers, commercial for buyers and sellers and so on. This is an "augmented" urban reality made of immaterial pixels that, by means of intelligent screens, video projections and interactive supports, meld with and add to the physical and material state of the traditional city. We surely must agree that, "architecture is no longer simply the play of masses in light. It now embraces the play of digital information in space."[11]

The interaction between real and virtual, between places in which our physical presence is needed and those where only an immaterial presence is necessary, is ever more prominent, and one aspect does not eliminate the other, but the two sit side by side and, in some way, together add power to "existential density." Tokyo, like other 21st-century cities, is resembling ever more closely a linked system of interacting, intelligent locations (both architectural and urban). The buildings, the *machines à habiter* of modernity, are ever more computers "à habiter," furnished with multiple processors, memories, control systems and networks. A large part of construction costs is eaten up by electronics. An intelligent software system that can periodically update itself is superimposed on the standard physical structure. And this is just as true, as we said early on, on the large territorial scale as it is on the small scale of furnishing and interior design.

Even clothing seems to be evolving towards a system of prostheses which can process data and supply services. Clothes and accessories are ever more densely populated with bits and bytes to guarantee health and

Night view

physical well-being, represent us and identify us, and enable us to communicate at a distance. This is the body electric, as prophesied by Walt Whitman, a body already up and running among the young Japanese, one ever more endowed with electronic prostheses, whose changed relationship with the world inevitably tends to change the way it relates to its mind too.

In terms of urban geometry, the attack on the Cartesian system translates into moving on from Euclidean space and embracing the more ample margins of freedom that topology allows. The key words are "fluidity," "viscosity" and "connection," coming within compositional logics tied to the universe of curves, rotations and folds in surfaces, and continual elastic transformations more or less metaphorically derived from the idea of complexity developed by Gilles Deleuze. In this complexity we find, significantly, the original meaning of "plexus": a weave, or physical or conceptual fold, a dynamic process of conformation. The grid of traditional western perspective is evolving into a net, into the oxymoron of a "three-dimensional surface," into a soft or "wet" grids, it is something that brings us back once more to liquid states: inconsistent, unstable, variable, and susceptible to continual transformations.

It is a sort of modernized Einfühlung's theory in which the sensitivity of curved lines in movement and their ability to interact by attraction or repulsion is obtained using a computer instead of the variable stroke of the designer's pen: prosthesis of the architect's creative thought on one side and machine as simple tool on the other. A strongly experimental process that will push us, as Deleuze might say, beyond the limit, beyond the point at which there begins a different state of being. A concept that, when examined closely, seems to make its mark on every manifestation of contemporary thinking, but also a challenge to the current marginality of architecture and to the confines—psychological as much as physical—that history is apparently assigning to it.

Tokyo today clearly demonstrates that all this can not but radically modify the thinking of planners, architects and everyone involved with the physical support of man's life. We must forget the city of history and accept the "e-topias," evolved urban systems networked with the rest of the planet that are anything but utopian, probably even "atopian." As Franco Purini wrote in the introduction to this volume, before us is the future's future.

[1] V. Gregotti, "Una modernità dis-orientata," in *Casabella*, no. 608-609, 1994.
[2] F. Maraini, *Ore Giapponesi*. Milan: Corbaccio, 2000, p. 112.
[3] A. Isozaki, "Città e architettura come rovina," in *Casabella*, no. 608-609, 1994.
[4] R. Barthes, *L'Empire des Signes*. Geneva: Skira, 1970.
[5] Z. Bauman, *Liquid Modernity*. Cambridge-Oxford: 2000.
[6] Ibid.
[7] J. Habermas, *Modernity – An Incomplete Project*, in *The Anti-Aesthetic, Essays on Postmodern Culture*, edited by H. Foster. Port Townsend: 1983, p.11.
[8] Z. Bauman, op. cit.
[9] J. Attali, *Chemins da sagesse: traité du labyrinthe*. Paris: 1996, p. 23.
[10] Cf. F. Tönnies, *Community and Association*. London: 1953. Or. Ed. 1887.
[11] W. Mitchell, *E-topia*. Cambridge (Ma)-London: The MIT Press, 1999, p. 41.

Dewhurst MacFarlane & Partners, entrance of Yurakucho Station, Marunouchi, Chiyoda-ku, 1999

Crossroads, Ginza, Chuo-ku

Taxis

Subway entrance,
Shibuya-ku

Escalator, Shibuya-ku

Makoto Sei Watanabe,
Iidabashi subway station,
2000
Ventilation towers studies

Makoto Sei Watanabe
Iidabashi subway station,
2000
Ventilation Towers

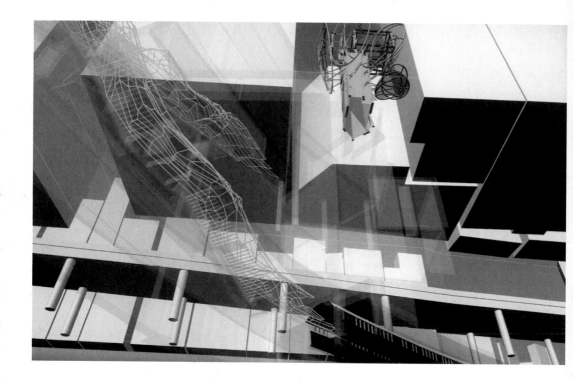

Subway station entrance,
Shinagawa-ku

Monorail

Outdoor escalator

Subway entrance

Subway station, Yokohama

Public phones

Offices

Vending machine

Clock at Narita airport

Electronic panel

Following pages:
Subway station

Index of Names

Photographic credits

Ando, Tadao: 139, 140, 141, 212 bottom.
Attoma Pepe, Beniamino: 15, 18, 25 bottom, 37 bottom, 108 top, 121 right, 122 right, 138, 194 bottom, 199 right, 200, 201, 217, 225, 229, 239 bottom left, 241 bottom.
Eisenman, Peter: 197, 198 top.
Ficco, Arcangelo: 170.
Foster, Norman: 180, 191.
Isozaki, Arata: 64, 158.
Kurokawa, Kisho: 67.
Mascarucci, Maria: 212 top right.
Mercuri, Franco: 17 bottom, 32, 69 top, 81, 84 right, 96 bottom right, 104 top and bottom right, 105 bottom, 106 right, 110, 111 left, 116, 122 left, 135, 154, 160, 174, 182, 188 right, 194 top left, 205 top, 208 top, 213, 220, 224, 226, 228, 234 bottom, 235 top, 238 bottom, 239 top and bottom right, 240 bottom.
Mori, Mariko: 28 top, 109 top.
Nikken Sekkei: 161 bottom.
Piano, Renzo: 70.
de Portzamparc, Christian: 190 right.
Remigio, Federica: 82, 84 left, 108 bottom, 111 right.
Rogers, Richard: 173, 198 bottom, 199 left.
Sacchi, Livio: 16 top, 17 top, 19, 22, 23, 24, 25 top, 26, 27, 28 bottom, 29, 30-31, 33, 34-35, 36, 37 centro, 66, 68, 71, 72 bottom, 87, 88-89, 91, 92, 93, 94, 95, 96 top, 97, 106 left, 115, 118 left, 120, 127 top, 128, 129, 136, 143, 150, 153 top, 155, 157, 158, 161 top, 162-163, 165, 167, 169, 171, 172, 175, 176-177, 178, 181, 183,

184-185, 186, 187, 188 left, 189, 190 left, 192, 194 top right, 195, 196, 199, 202-203, 204, 205 bottom, 206 right, 207, 209 bottom, 211, 212 top left, 214-215, 216, 231, 233, 234 top, 237, 240 top, 241 top, 242-243.
Sierri, Elena: 16 bottom, 21, 69 bottom, 72 top left e right, 107, 133, 153 bottom, 222, 235 bottom, 238 top.
Tange, Kenzō: 59, 61, 62.
Tzokas, Athanasios: 20, 96 bottom left, 105 top, 166, 168, 221, 227.
Villari, Alessandro: 104 bottom left, 109 bottom, 118 right, 145, 146, 147, 148, 149, 151, 152, 164, 209.
Watanabe, Makoto Sei: 236.